Cheiro, whose real name was Count Louis Hamon, was born in 1866. He wrote his first book on palmistry at the age of twelve, expanding his career as an author to include ghost stories, occultism and Hollywood scenarios.

Widely travelled, he worked as a press correspondent during the Japan-Chinese War and the Russo-Japanese War. He was also a founder member of the Pacific-Geographic Society and a Fellow of the Royal Geographic Society. He died in 1936.

# *You and Your Hand*

**CHEIRO**

Revised by Louise Owen

SPHERE BOOKS LIMITED
30/32 Gray's Inn Road, London WC1X 8JL

First published in Great Britain by Jarrolds Ltd, 1932
This edition revised by Louise Owen and reset 1969
Revisions and this arrangement copyright © Jarrolds Ltd. 1969
Published by Sphere Books 1974
Reprinted 1977

TRADE
MARK

Printed in Great Britain by
Hazell Watson & Viney Ltd
Aylesbury, Bucks

# Contents

# You and Your Hand

# Reviser's note

As a teacher of cheirology for the Society for the Study of Physiological Patterns (S.S.P.P.), it is my practice to advise students to read Cheiro's later books in conjunction with my lessons. I was therefore delighted when Jarrolds decided to publish a revised version of Cheiro's last book on palmistry, *You and Your Hand*, and very pleased to have the opportunity to assist in the work of revision.

Cheiro combined the best of palmistry's folklore with his own opinions and deductions gained through years of experience. He eliminated the surrounding aura of mystery and magic and lifted palmistry out of the tents and booths of the gypsy and vagabond to the realms of serious study. In doing this he performed a great service to the study of the human hand, leading the way to the present-day scientific and psychological approach to palmistry.

He wrote his books so that all could read and understand, outlining the basic principles clearly and positively, in plain terms. His system of presentation makes it easy for the student to grasp the essentials of the study. In fact most writers on the subject since Cheiro's time have followed his system and basic principles, adapting them to present-day requirements.

Cheiro was, of course, a Victorian and wrote in the style of his age when class distinctions and melodrama were accepted. This should be taken into account by the student. The paragraph referring to the Seamstress and the Lady has been retained for its sheer Victorianism—also the many references to the 'Murderer's Mark', 'Murderer's Thumb', poisoners, etc. These may seem a trifle melodramatic, but in view of the violence of our own times such references give rise to speculation on the signs to be found in the hands of the cold-blooded, brutal raiders and murderers who use sawn-off shotguns and other terrible weapons. One should also consider Cheiro's remarks about drug addiction!

For easier reading and study, certain cuts have been made to avoid unnecessary repetition and subjects outside the scope of palmistry have been eliminated. This reduces Cheiro's Fore-word to a certain extent, but his outline of the history of palmistry has been retained as being of value to the student.

The instructions for taking hand prints have been brought up-to-date and a footnote has been added.

Part II in the old edition is now Part I because this is the more logical arrangement, leading to the study of the lines in relation to the type of hand in which they are placed.

An insertion has been made before the section dealing with the minor marks and signs because the original drawings were too geometrical and because an explanation of how these marks are formed and of their actual appearance would be of service to those who are new to the study of palmistry.

For easier reference, all the drawn illustrations have been re-numbered running in sequence right through the book, and this applies also to the reproductions of actual hand prints.

There has been no major revision of Cheiro's text for it is his book, and although it might be termed a 'period piece', his findings are still the basis for modern study and research on the nature of man.

L.O.

1969

# Author's foreword

This book will probably be the last I shall ever write on the study of hands.

After more than forty years of professional work and investigation of this subject in Europe and America, the 'hour-glass of time' warns me to be prepared to give the final results of my investigations to humanity at large.

Believing as I do, and having proved by extensive experience the value of this study for parents who wish to give every possible advantage to their children, I shall explain as simply as I can the indications of character and mentality as shown by the shape and nature of the hand, and by the lines written on the palm.

Although my other works on this subject published at various times throughout my career have dealt with it thoroughly, and have met with unusual acknowledgment and approbation, there is a difference between this book and all the others. It is probably my last book on the subject, and for that reason will not only contain the foundation on which my previous works were compiled, but will give the finishing-touches to that study of humanity I have made so peculiarly my own.

This work is not a mere copy of my former books, no

matter how explanatory they may have been, but contains original and fresh matter drawn from years of more advanced experience—the result being, I humbly submit, the most complete and extensive work that has ever been given to the world on a subject of interest and advantage to all classes.

'Forewarned is forearmed!'—words of more force and meaning today than ever before. The 'battle of life' is *not* becoming more easy. The struggle for survival grows *more* intense day by day. Therefore a study that can help men and women to know themselves—realise their weakness and recognise their successful tendencies—must be *of inestimable importance to those who would succeed.*

There is a logical reason for the lines of the hand telling the story of life with unfailing accuracy, and this will be subsequently explained. I must, however, say *en passant* that this study is only one more of the many books of nature where God writes in history on leaves, on stones and on everything.

I am not attempting to make my readers believe in something that is based on superstition. Contrary to common conception, the study of the hand has occupied some of the greatest minds in all ages. Its beginnings are lost in the night of antiquity that has no dawn.

In all countries, in all civilisations, the study of the hand has always been associated with the study of life itself. Thousands of years before Christ, the Chinese carved the hand and its mysterious lines on their monuments and temples. So did the Japanese, the Persians and the Hindus.

Authentic records exist in various libraries in the world which prove that such studies as astrology and palmistry have their origin in the farthest dawn of time.

Out of astrology was born the study of the hand. It was found that persons who had the planet Jupiter in a powerful position in the horoscope had the same qualities expressed by the first finger of the hand having the base or mount under it large or well developed. If this finger was short or crooked and the mount under it hollow or depressed, the planet Jupiter held an inferior position in the horoscope.

In the course of time the first finger became designated as

'the finger of Jupiter', the second that of Saturn and so on with the other fingers and mounts of the palm.

Even the most casual student of this study is aware that if what is called the Mount of Venus (the ball of the thumb), is found large or well developed, the sensual side of the nature will be more in evidence than when this portion of the palm is flat or depressed in appearance.

This point alone is borne out by medical science, which demonstrates that what is known as the 'great palmar arch' or main blood vessel from the body passes under this part of the palm. Consequently if this blood vessel is extra large, the Mount of Venus is more developed. One draws the inference, therefore, that when the force or strength of the body is unusual, the passionate tendencies will be more in evidence—sensuality being largely dependent on robust physical health and strong circulation of the blood.

The study of the thumb alone goes far to prove that palmistry is a natural science built on observation and genuine research. The famous French scientist and writer, d'Arpentigny, said: 'the thumb individualises the man'.

Sir Charles Bell has in his works called attention to the fact that on the paw or hand of the chimpanzee, which is the nearest approach to the human, the thumb—although well formed in every way—does not reach the base of the first finger. The deduction therefore is, that the longer and better formed the thumb, the more the man has developed beyond the brute creation.

The most casual observation will prove this to be so. A man with a short, clumsy-looking, thick-set thumb will be coarse and brutish in his nature, while a man or woman with a long, well-formed thumb will have highly developed intellectual faculties, backed up by strong will and determination.

A visit to a mental hospital is an illuminating lesson to the student. Here the weak-looking, badly formed thumbs of some of the inmates will convince him of the important relation of this member of the hand to character.

It is to the far-famed ancient Greek civilisation that we owe the foundation of what I may call the more practical and advanced side of the study of the hand.

History records that many of the most celebrated of the Greek philosophers not only practised this study themselves, but also taught it to their pupils. The ancient Greek civilisation is still considered the highest and most intellectual the world has ever known. It is significant that it was in such surroundings that palmistry or Cheiromancy—from the Greek word *Cheir*, the hand—found favour in the eyes of those highly cultivated philosophers whose works and teachings are perpetuated today in all of the great universities and colleges of the world.

Again going back to history, we find that Hispanus discovered on an altar dedicated to Hermes, a book on Cheiromancy written in letters of gold. This he sent as a present to the world-conqueror, Alexander the Great, as 'a study worthy the attention of an elevated and inquiring mind'.

History also informs us that this study of the hand was practised by such philosophers as Pythagoras, Aristotle, Anaxagoras; also by Paracelsus, Pliny, Cardamis, Albertus Magnus, and the Emperor Augustus.

All this goes to prove that the study in question is not only one of the most ancient in the world, but one that has occupied the serious attention of the most exalted minds in history.

Students in modern times, therefore, need not be ashamed or discouraged if in following it they encounter the sneers of the ignorant, who—having no idea of the noble record of ancient lineage that lies behind it—class the science as something to be tabooed, or not worthy of their 'superior intelligence'.

I will touch on the reason for the study of Cheiromancy falling into disrepute during the Middle Ages, not only as a matter of interest for the ordinary reader, but for the benefit of the student who is entitled to know the history of the subject he endeavours to master.

Unfortunately the statement has to be made that the power of the Church has always been directed against any form of knowledge not sponsored by itself. In the first place, the study of the hand was considered by the fathers of the Church to be the 'child of pagans', and consequently of doubtful origin.

It also embodied Fate or Predestination, which was totally in opposition to the earlier doctrines of the Church, although in later years the Episcopalian branch laid down in its 17th Article of Religion that 'predestination to life is the everlasting purpose of God'.

So determined became the prejudice against the idea of knowledge being derived from a study of the hand, that the translators of the Bible mistranslated the seventh verse of the thirty-seventh chapter of Job. In the original Hebrew this verse reads: 'God placed signs and marks in the hands of all the sons of men that all men might know their works.' In the English version that is mistranslated to read: 'God sealed up the hands of men that all men may know God's works.'

This verse, about the middle of the 16th century, caused one of the most important discussions among theologians that has ever taken place, some of the greatest thinkers of that age, such as Franciscus Valesius, Schultens, Lyrannus and Debreo, advocating that the verse should read that the lines of the hand were placed there that 'all men might know their works'. In spite of such opposition by these authorities, the mistranslation remained in the English version, while in many others the verse was suppressed altogether.

About this period the Church started a vigorous crusade against all manuscripts or books that in any way dealt with what was called 'hidden knowledge', otherwise occultism in any form whatever.

The order was given out in all churches and in all countries that any person possessing manuscripts or books, on such a 'subject of the Devil' as palmistry, astrology, alchemy, or magic, was to hand over such things to the priests and have them destroyed or burned in the public square. Failure to obey this order was punishable by death—any person afterwards discovered in possession of such books being burned alive at the stake.

The result of such a drastic order was that most priceless manuscripts and books on such subjects were destroyed—or lost. By 'lost' I mean withdrawn from the public, for in many cases the priests kept the most valuable for themselves. Even tually the greater part reached the library of the Vatican in Rome, where some hundreds of volumes on astrology, occultism and palmistry may be found in the present day.

In England, not only was this order carried out with the utmost severity, but about this time Henry VIII proclaimed himself 'Father of the English Church', and had an Act of Parliament passed against all 'Palmists, Astrologers, Witches and Workers of the Devil', condemning all such as 'rogues and vagabonds', to lose their possessions, to stand one year in the public pillory, and then be expelled from the country. Perhaps this much-married monarch was afraid his wives might learn their fate.

On the death of Queen Elizabeth, James the First came to the throne, and commenced at once a campaign against palmists, astrologers, witches, and as his Act of Parliament adds: 'all who traffic with the Devil'.

This Act is still in force. It was actively revived during the reigns of the various Georges, also under Queen Victoria, King Edward VII, and King George V. Palmists have been prosecuted all over the country, and in many cases sent to prison.*

It is reasonable to suppose that every portion of the brain, like every other living organism, is in a continual state of evolution and change. These changes must alter and affect the brain cells, and through them the nerve system of the entire body, especially those to the lines of the hand.

Therefore it follows that a man or woman at, say, twenty years of age, may commence some new development of thought or education which is fated to alter his or her entire course of life at forty or fifty as the case may be. At twenty the change has *already commenced* in the brain, and may even then, by affecting the brain cells, have registered its effect in the nerve system and more particularly on the nerve-connections between the brain and the hand.

---

* The new Act of 1951 repeals the ancient Witchcraft Act of 1735, and makes substitutions for certain provisions of section S.4 of the Vagrancy Act of 1824, but the position of all who practise palmistry and the associated arts remains uncertain.—L.O

Medical science has demonstrated that by generations of continual use, the nerves from the brain to the hand have become extra highly developed; that the hand, whether passive or active, *is in every sense the immediate servant of the brain.*

Sir Charles Bell states: 'in the examination of a skeleton a zoologist recognises that the inequalities and ridges found upon the surface of the bones are the result of the action and pressure of muscles and nerves' From the broken fragment of a bone a scientist can build up the entire structure and proportions of the dead animal; its race, habits, and even the diseases it would be liable to suffer from.

If such, as has been proved, can be done from the fragment of a bone, from this standpoint alone, how much, I ask, may we not do by a careful study of that most important member of the body—the hand?

Is there anything ridiculous, then, in the idea that the hand specialist—as the true palmist is—should be able to describe the health, the surroundings of the past and present, and even the probabilities of the future, from an examination of the hand independent of any other theory?

That the lines on the palm are not made by work can easily be proved by the simplest consideration on the part of the ordinary observer.

If they were made by work, a seamstress folding her hands some thousands of times a day in pursuit of her work should logically have more lines on her palm than the society woman of leisure. The exact opposite, however, is the case. The seamstress becomes a mere machine, not increasing the number of lines on the hand, while the woman of luxury and ease, having an active brain (even if it may be only occupied by organising garden parties, dinners and dances), *will have hundreds more lines than her more mechanical sister.*

There is still another theory that may be the solution of it all—it is that of the 'sub-conscious' brain—the mystery by which science explains the inexplicable, without being able to solve it

This theory may be rejected by what is called abstract science, but that is no reason why it should not be true. Science with all its research has never yet discovered *what life is*. It has still to answer a thousand and one questions that humanity asks concerning the common things of day to day.

My own view, which I present for what it is worth, is that what is called fate may exist on broad lines as may be exemplified by the rise and fall of nations, through great wars, great catastrophes and such like causes affecting humanity in masses. But as good and evil are the balancing poles in nature, so is knowledge the equallising poise in destiny, whereby the God-like power of will or mind may be called into play, to work with or against fate, as the case may be. One example of what I mean may suffice.

An engine-driver may receive a warning in advance that a broken bridge some ten or twenty miles ahead spells catastrophe for himself and the train he is driving. If he is a sensible man he will accept the warning—wait for the bridge to be repaired—and so save his life and the lives of others. If, on the contrary, he is too stupid or headstrong to be guided by the knowledge he has gained he will dash on to destruction.

I cannot give a better illustration of what this study of the hand can do in giving advance warnings of broken bridges on life's track than the following story:

During my first season in London I read Oscar Wilde's hands from behind curtains at a large reception. He was then at the very height of his fame. I told him his Lines of Fate and Success were broken just seven years further on. Instead of taking the warning, he turned and announced gravely to the assembled guests: 'Cheiro may be right. As fate keeps no road-menders on her highways—*Che Sara Sara*—what is to be will be.'

This otherwise clever man could not realise that the '*road-mender*' was in himself. He made no change in his habits and so he went headlong to his doom.

Against this example I have seen many others who have taken warning of the 'broken road', pulled up in time, saved themselves and in many cases others with them.

It is here that this study would be of inestimable value if used by parents to find out the hidden tendencies of their children. Not only might they be able to save their loved ones from wasting endless years in pursuit of some career that could never bring success, but they could avert the heart-ache of uncongenial work followed *because a child's parents or grand-parents had made a success in that particular kind of work.*

How often do parents see a loved child grow up the 'square peg in the round hole' they put him in, and blame God or fate for the failure.

In hundreds of cases narrow-mindedness or religious prejudice has prevented parents from taking advantage of the warnings that this study could place at their disposal.

In regard to such matters as health and inherited or incipient disease, I know of no study that can give such accurate warnings of not only the nature of the malady, but also the date—often long years in advance—when, if the warning is not taken, it may be too late to combat the danger.

In all such cases the 'broken bridge' might have been repaired—but those terrible words 'too late' too often turn life into a tragedy instead of the beautiful creation it might have been.

In the following pages of this work it will be my privilege to give many illustrations of 'broken roads or bridges' that it has been my lot to meet with in my long professional experience.

CHEIRO

1932

*Part 1*   Cheirognomy

## Chapter 1 The shapes of hands, fingers and nails

The study of the hand is divided into two sections, Cheiromancy—the lines on the palm, and Cheirognomy—the shape of the hands and fingers.

The first is the more intimate as it relates to the hidden qualities and destiny of each person, while the latter denotes the breeding, racial and more general characteristics.

The various shapes of hands and their suitability to various walks in life or occupations is well worthy of observation and study.

A man who is a judge of horses can tell by a glance at the limbs of the animal what class of work it is built for. He would not think for one moment of expecting from a Clydesdale the speed of a race-horse, and so on.

In the same way the student of the shapes of hands should be able from a glance at the formation to place his subject in a certain class, and would not expect the same quality or type of mental work from a person with short stubby hands as from a man with long beautifully formed ones.

There are seven distinct types of hands:
1. The elementary—or lowest type.
2. The square—or useful hand.

3. The spatulate—or active nervous type.
4. The philosophic—or knotty.
5. The conic—or artistic.
6. The psychic—or idealistic.
7. The mixed type.

In civilised races the elementary or lowest type is rarely found.

The square hand is the most usual, and this again is likely to be found with fingers taking on some resemblance to any one of the seven types.

## Chapter 2    The elementary hand

The elementary hand (Fig. 1) in appearance is short, stubby and clumsy-looking, with a thick heavy palm, short stubby fingers and short badly formed nails.

In Dr. Cairn's well-known work on the *Physiognomy of the Human Body*, he states that 'the bones of the palm form, among brute animals, almost the whole hand'.

The deduction to be drawn therefore is that the more the palm appears to dominate the hand, the more the animal nature will be in evidence.

Persons possessing the elementary hand have low mental capacity. As a general rule very few lines are found on such hands, those seen being the Lines of Life, Heart and Head. The latter is generally short and coarse looking.

The thumb is usually thick-set and short, hardly reaching to the base of the first finger; the nail phalange is square, short and thick.

Such a type of hand indicates a slow thinker, devoid of ambition, shrewd in some ways where his immediate material interest is concerned, but unable to grasp any ideas not related to his own environment. Generally stolid, he can be roused to sudden fury when goaded beyond his own understanding.

He is guided by emotion and instinct and understands only the fundamentals of life. He is not necessarily an unhappy man.

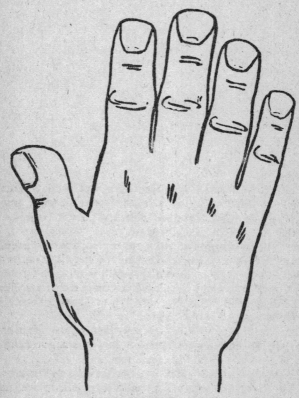

FIG. 1. THE ELEMENTARY HAND

The square, useful or practical hand as it is called, is distinctly square in its appearance. It looks square across the wrist, across the base of the fingers, and the very ends of the fingers and nails appear square (Fig. 2).

This type of hand belongs to level-headed, practical people, and is more generally found as the predominant class in all business communities.

Persons with this type have fixed conventional views. They are great respecters of law and authority and are methodical in their habits.

They are orderly in all they do, they have a place for everything and everything in its place—not only in their households, but in their brains.

They are not quarrelsome, but can be very obstinate and determined in their views. They love logic and reason, and look with suspicion on any theory their minds cannot grasp.

They are neither adaptable to people nor to new ideas. They think slowly along practical lines. They generally speak slowly and ponderously as if they must weigh each word.

They are patient and obedient to those above them. For this reason they make excellent soldiers of the 'rank and file' class, also good government servants.

They are not demonstrative in affection but are sincere and reliable in friendship.

Their greatest fault is that they are inclined to measure everything by a 'twelve-inch rule', and disbelieve all they cannot understand.

On such hands as a general rule there are very few lines—

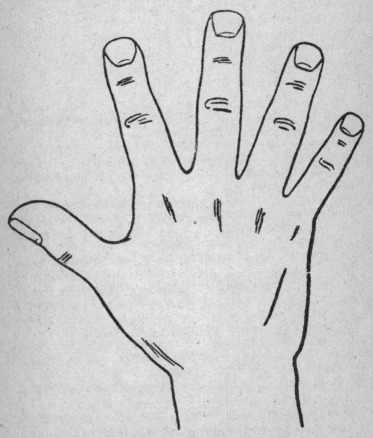

FIG. 2. THE SQUARE HAND

just the principal ones. The Line of Head, as may be expected with this type, is level and straight but usually short. If it should slope downwards even in the slightest degree it gives a longing and desire for art or imaginative things, quite out of keeping with the basic character. In such cases the practical hard-headed business man, when he has made money and feels himself secure, will be found buying pictures and works of art for his home or office, not because he understands them, but to satisfy the yearning of his sloping head line for something from the world of imagination.

### The square hand with short square fingers

This class of hand is quite a common one to find and is easily recognised. The palm looks more important than the fingers, which are often short and blunt looking.

With such a type one meets the true materialist, the man with no vision, no ideality, the real 'doubting Thomas' of life. The man who cannot honestly believe unless he feels the 'flesh and blood' of reality.

On the hand of such a man it would be rare to find anything but the three principal Lines of Life, Head and Heart. If the other lines are there they are generally so slight and faint that it is often difficult to see them.

Such a man believes in nothing outside of himself, he denies all spiritual things, it is quite in keeping with his type that he may not believe in a deity. There is one god, however, that he does worship, the God of Gold. This type slowly and steadily accumulates wealth, not by any great talent or merit, but by plodding perseverance and dogged determination.

### The square hand with long square fingers

This type denotes a higher development of mentality. If I may express it, the nature with its longer fingers, as it were, reaches out to grasp the things of the intellectual world, and at the same time applies facts, reason and logic to all its pursuits.

With a good or long Head Line on this type of hand, one

has met the man who can become the scientist, the doctor, the surgeon, the analytical lawyer or judge.

A man who, although he may have to submit everything to reason or scientific examination, can reach beyond the purely material.

### The square hand with knotty or philosophic fingers

This type of hand is nearly always found with long fingers, but with knotty joints. It denotes a class of mind still higher than the previous type. It is practical and philosophical at the same time.

The possessors of this hand make excellent architects, mathematicians and research workers in scientific pursuits. They usually choose some profession in preference to a business life. They do not love wealth or amass it like those who have the type of square hand I previously described. They are great readers of deep literature, and usually write well themselves on whatever subject they make a special study.

### The square hand with spatulate fingers

The fingers of this type are called spatulate on account of being broad at the ends like a spatula. They are irregular in appearance—often look as if they were disjointed, generally very supple and are easily bent backwards.

Persons possessing this type are original and inventive, but from a practical foundation owing to the palm being square.

Their inventions have more or less a useful bent—machines to save labour of all sorts, such as agricultural machinery, weaving, spinning, printing and so forth. They also excel in engineering and in the execution of large projects. They do not know what the word 'impossible' means.

If a long Head Line is found on the hands of this type, their plans will turn out well. If the Line of Head is short and coarse, they will be erratic and not able to bring their inventive ideas to completion.

## *The square hand with conic fingers*

This apparent contradiction in types produces a combination of the practical with the artistic, thus giving to the latter a greater chance of success than if the entire hand were purely conic or artistic.

This blend of two opposite types, curiously as it might appear at first sight, produces the class of disposition that can excel in music or in composition of music, or in literature.

The logical reason for this is that the square hand in itself represents practicality and level-headedness, a balance necessary for the emotional artistic temperament of the musician, composer or writer.

The square hand gives the power of application and the methodical perseverance absolutely necessary to support the inspirational faculties of the musician.

The brain of the composer creates from the solid foundation of harmony and counter-point, the tones and semi-tones of fantasy. From the known his spirit enters the gates of the unknown where his dreams become realities, his visions so tangible that he lifts humanity with himself into the heaven of ideality.

The practical foundation of the square hand with conic fingers is useful for literary people in the same way as for musicians and composers. It gives a solid foundation on which to build the superstructure of imagination. For this reason the square palm with conic fingers is usually found among writers as well as musicians; in the latter case the conic fingers are generally more or less of the spatulate formation at the nail phalange.

## *The square hand with psychic fingers*

This type is extremely rarely found as the combination is too contradictory. If it should be met with, it denotes extreme ideality coming in moments of impulse out of a practical nature, but as a general rule the disposition is too full of contradictions to be successful.

## *The square hand with mixed fingers*

This type is quite often met with. It consists of some of the fingers being different in shape, or in many cases every one may be different.

A usual formation is that the first may appear long, rounded and pointed at the end as if it were a finger belonging to the conic type, the second or finger of Saturn may be distinctly square, the third spatulate and the fourth philosophic or even psychic, with the thumb supple or double jointed.

Such a mixed hand would indicate versatility of ideas or talents, ranging from the inspirational to the scientific, a person who could discuss almost any subjec twith the greatest facility.

The fault in such cases is a tendency to lack continuity of purpose unless the Head Line shows some unusual mental determination or will power.

From these examples will be seen the widely divergent shades of character that may be found in each person.

This type is called spatulate, not only on account of the tip of each finger making the appearance of a spatula such as used in chemists' mortars, but also because the palm, instead of having the appearance of being square like the previous type, is often broad at the wrist or base, or at the upper part of the base of the fingers (Fig. 3).

When the greater width is at the wrist, the palm becomes more or less inclined or sloping towards the base of the fingers. On the contrary, when the greatest width is shown under the fingers the shape then slopes back to the wrist.

I will now explain the meaning of the spatulate hand itself, and go into the above distinctions later.

The spatulate hand, when firm and hard, denotes a nature whose base is the exact opposite to the methodical characteristics given by the square type. The spatulate, being more or less erratic, highly strung, excitable and restless, is the hand of energy, activity, unconventionality, originality and invention.

It is for this reason that this type, when accentuated, is called the 'hand of the crank'. A straight, level-looking Head Line on such a hand will keep the above characteristics within bounds, but as a rule with such a type as the spatulate, the Line of Head will be found, even when long, of a wavy or up and down formation.

It must always be borne in mind that the distinctive attribute of the spatulate hand is its intense love of action, energy and independence.

It is the hand of the inventor, the engineer of large daring and original plans, the pioneer, navigator, explorer. Its most distinctive characteristic is its love of independence both in thought and action—the hand of the man who will not follow the conventional in anything he undertakes.

No matter in what class of life the spatulate hand finds itself, it will in one form or another assert its right to develop a distinct individuality of its own.

A doctor, lawyer, writer, scientist, preacher, actor or statesman who has the spatulate type of hand will break all rules of precedent, not for the sake of being eccentric, or out of the common, but because of his independence and originality of thought.

It is from this hand that the world gets its army of men and women it is often pleased to call 'cranks' simply because such individuals cannot follow the rut made by the centuries of sheep that have passed before them.

Such types are often the 'advance agents' of thought, those who are 'born before their time'—the heralds of new ideas from which others later on reap the advantage.

When the spatulate hand is soft and flabby, the qualities I have described are more inclined to be dormant, or *in the mind* instead of *in actuality*. In other words the person has the ideas and desires without the power to express them, the softness or flabbiness of the nature militating against the hard work necessary for the execution of his desires.

Curiously enough persons with the spatulate hand soft and flabby are usually irritable and fretful in disposition, perhaps because at heart they feel their inability to produce or make manifest the work belonging to their type.

I will now explain the meaning of the two types of the formation of the spatulate palm that I alluded to at the commencement of the chapter.

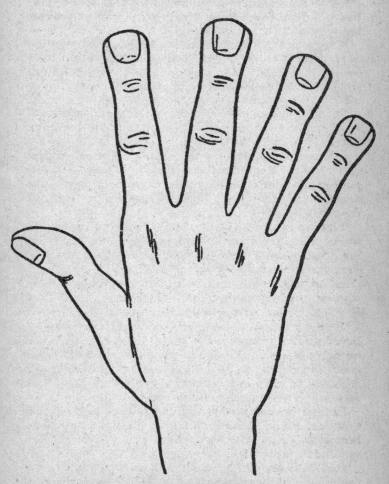

FIG. 3. THE SPATULATE HAND

The broad development at the base of the fingers is the more practical of the two. If the man be an inventor, he will use his talents in the domain of useful inventions such as in connection with labour-saving instruments or machines of practical everyday use to humanity.

If the angular or broad development be at the wrist, his inventions will relate more to the visionary side of life. Such a man may produce equally great ideas or inventions, but he will be more likely to be far ahead of his time.

The word 'philosophic' is derived from the Greek *philos*—love, and *sophia*—wisdom.

When the ancient Greek civilisation was at its highest, its teachers and sages observed that persons whose hands had very decided joints separating the phalanges of the fingers had a more thoughtful, reflective or introspective type of mind than persons having the joints less pronounced, or, in other words, smooth—as the greater majority of people have.

After we know not how many ages of observation, they noticed that those who possessed smooth fingers acted more impulsivlely on their decisions, while those with pronounced divisions or joints came to conclusions after greater thoughtfulness or reflection.

These latter types it was also observed had a more philosophic outlook on life in general. In consequence this very distinct class of hand became known as 'the philosophic'.

The formation of this hand is easily recognised. It is long, angular, with long fingers, developed joints and generally a longer-looking finger-nail or nail phalange than that belonging to the square hand (Fig. 4).

As far as success in the form of worldly possessions is con-

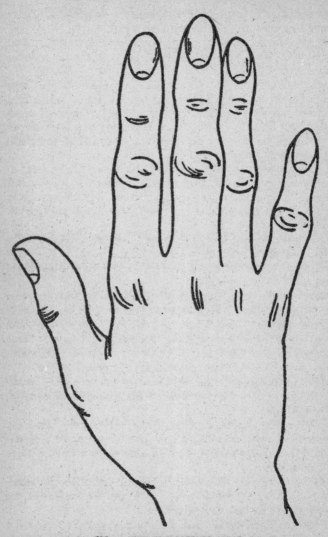

FIG. 4. THE PHILOSOPHIC HAND

cerned it is not a favourable type to have. Its possessors may accumulate wisdom, but rarely, if ever, gold.

Persons with the philosophic type are deep thinkers and students in whatever line of work they make their own particular study.

Among them may be found Egyptologists, delvers into antiquities in all lands, investigators of signs, symbols and dead languages, theologians, doctors of philosophy, professors in colleges, botanists, research chemists, writers on abstruse subjects—all the great variety of thinkers who live in the world of theory rather than of practice.

In the mysterious design of human existence they appear to have been created as a balance against sordid materialism of all kinds. This type of hand has given to the world the hermit, the recluse, the ascetic—and it may be found in all lands in all grades of society.

It is more often found in Oriental countries, especially in India and the Far East where the philosophic mind has more suitable soil and conditions for its growth and development.

Nearer home in the United States, England and Europe, this type of hand made itself manifest in such men as Abraham Lincoln, Longfellow, Emerson, Shelley, Browning and Tennyson—in such men as Cardinal Newman, Cardinal Manning and the late Pope Leo XIII, all of which had the philosophic type of hand in the most marked degree.

In that famous painting of 'hands in prayer' by Albrecht Dürer, one can see the mystic asceticism of this type expressed in every line.

In character the possessors of the philosophic hand are inclined to be secretive and silent—deep thinkers, careful and analytical in their thoughts and expressions, even in their use of little words.

Such people are difficult to understand or approach. Sensitive to the highest degree they shrink into themselves at the approach of rudeness or idle curiosity.

They are dignified and proud in their way, but theirs is the pride of being different from the vulgar herd, of being priests in the holy sanctuary of the mind where only the true worshipper can gain admittance.

As the philosophic type has the underlying quality of the fatalist, the Line of Fate on the hand is generally clearly and distinctly marked.

In such hands it is not as a rule a heavy line. It has seldom any branches or influence lines—just a fine thread as it were of destiny linking the cradle to the grave and nothing more.

On such hands the Line of Sun is rarely seen. Men and women belonging to the philosophic type care little for fame, glory or the plaudits of the public. Their reward is within themselves—the reward of achievement—of having done conscientious work for the higher advancement of their fellow beings.

# *Chapter 6*   The conic or artistic hand

The conic hand is also called the artistic on account of its beautiful shape and rounded tapering fingers (Fig. 5).

Its possessors love form, colour and artistic things of every description, although often without the creative instinct in themselves. If they do work at art in any form such as painting, drawing, designing, music or literature, they usually only do so on the impulse of the moment and lack continuity of purpose.

They are as a rule extremely versatile in their ideas, and nearly always do a little of everything and nothing extremely well unless the Line of Head is very decidedly marked.

This hand is usually found round, full and soft. The firm type is the better of the two and gives more promise of success.

The conic type appears to greater advantage in company, especially that of strangers whom they have met for the first time. They love the glitter and dazzle of entertainment, balls, dances and dinners. They are good conversationalists, can talk on any subject, but are more or less superficial in knowledge.

They have not the depth of the student, through their want of application. They employ impulse rather than reason, instinct in place of knowledge. Their brilliancy of talk hides many defects and they are always considered good company and 'the life of the party'.

FIG    THE CONIC OR ARTISTIC HAND

In matters of affection they are extremely impressionable, but changeable and bored if they see too much of one person. As a rule they are easily offended and quick-tempered, but anger does not last long with such natures. They speak out what is on their minds hastily, but are too indolent or luxury-loving to keep up the fight for any length of time.

They are curiously selfish *where their own personal comfort is concerned*, yet generous in money matters and easily imposed on through their emotions.

They are much affected by their surroundings and the conditions under which they may be forced to live. They rise to the greatest heights of rapture or descend to the lowest depths of despair over trifles that other types would hardly notice. They are more easily influenced by colour, music, eloquence, tears, joys, sorrows than any other class.

If, however, the conic hand is firm or elastic and the Head Line is strongly marked, especially if it appears straight or level, the women of this type rise in life, and reign as queens as long as their beauty and charm last. It is the class of Head Line that decides the success of this type more than anything else.

When the Line of Head on such hands appears with an open space between it and the Line of Life, they are ambitious and have a keen sense of the dramatic in all they do. For perhaps this reason this type is largely found among actresses or singers of the emotional class.

It must not be forgotten, however, that such people depend more on the inspirational mood of the moment than on serious study or application. The orator with such a type of hand will sway multitudes by his flow of eloquence and dramatic power. A good example of this type was William Jennings Bryan, who was called the 'silver-tongued' orator of the United States. He had beautifully formed conic hands with a long Line of Head from under the base of the first finger and slightly sloping towards the Mount of Luna, or, as it is often designated, the Mount of Imagination.

It must always be borne in mind that the type of hand relates to the *natural* temperament of the individual—it is the foundation, as it were, on which one builds.

A woman with a more square type, especially if she has the conic fingers, can be equally as great an actress or singer as one with the purely conic foundation, but she will achieve her success by a different method, by application, study and perseverance— by the greater powers of endurance and patience she possesses.

Study and genius divide equally between them the ladder of fame. Genius often sits on the steps to dream. Study works and rises rung by rung. It is only the earthworms dazzled by the heights above them who confound the two and often crown study with the laurels of genius.

On the conic hand, the Lines of Fate and Sun usually appear more prominent than on the other types, as such people are more the 'children of fate' than the makers of destiny.

# Chapter 7    The psychic hand

The most beautiful of all hands in appearance, but the most unfortunate of all from a worldly standpoint, is what is known as the psychic type (Fig. 6).

The name explains itself—that which appertains to the soul.

The very word recalls to one's mind the old legend of the envy of the Goddess Venus—the goddess of passion—against the more spiritual charm of the daughter of the soul.

In our present civilisation a pure type is very difficult to find. Its dreamy chastity and mental spirituality is not sought after by our present-day sons of earth. But although the highest expression of this class of hand may be hard to find, there are numbers of men and women who approach it so closely that they must be taken into consideration.

In formation, this type is long, narrow and slender, with long tapering fingers, pointed tips and almond-shaped nails.

Its very fineness and beauty indicate its want of strength and energy—it is not fitted for the roughness of the battle of life. Those persons who have the psychic hand or the nearest approach to it, have the purely visionary idealistic nature, gentle in manner, slow to anger, confiding and trustful—they are easily deceived, imposed upon and ruined.

They have no idea how to be business-like, practical or

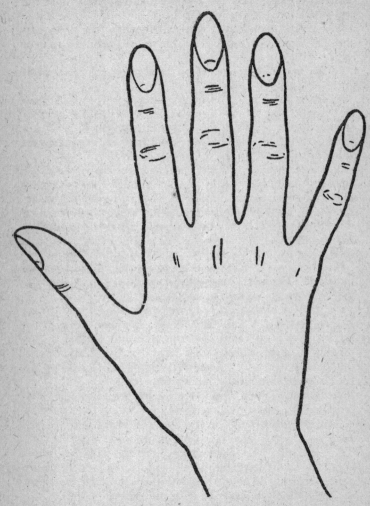

IG. 6. THE PSYCHIC HAND

worldly They are easily influenced by others, love the wrong people and end life in such a tangle that only death itself can untie the knot.

This type is consciously or unconsciously a deeply religious one. The devotional and the emotional are the under-tones of their souls.

All forms of ceremonial, magic and mystery call to them out of the unknown.

They are 'sensitive' in the purest meaning of the word. They 'feel' things, yet cannot define their feelings—dreamers of dreams, they cannot translate them into language. They are misunderstood by both parents and people, and the loneliness of life eats like wormwood into their hearts.

As a rule the Line of Head on the psychic hand clings too closely to that of Life, denying them the self-confidence they need so much. It is also generally found sloping down towards the Mount of the Imagination, or in the worst cases remaining very close to the Line of Life, and circling as it were under the Mount of Luna—as is shown on the impression of a suicide's hand (Plate 6).

In such a case if the hand is a woman's she feels so utterly unfitted to hold her own in life that to escape from herself she often flies to the peace of the unknown.

The mixed hand is so called because it cannot be classed as square, spatulate, conic, philosophic or psychic. The fingers also appear to belong to different types, one may be pointed, one square, one spatulate, one philosophic, etc. (Fig. 7).

Men or women who possess the mixed hand are full of versatility, and generally suffer from changeability of purpose. They are adaptable to people and circumstances and also to the various kinds of work they may find offered to them. If, however, a strong level-looking Line of Head be found on such a hand, the owner will have as much change of success as any other.

Persons who have the mixed hand are so adaptable to circumstances that they never feel the ups and downs of fortune like other people—also almost all kinds or conditions of work come easy to them.

They find life so interesting and full of change that with all their ups and downs of fortune they rarely, if ever, commit suicide.

On the mixed hand, the Lines of Fate and Sun are usually very clearly shown, and such persons are most decidedly believers in fate, luck and chance.

It is quite usual to find this type inveterate gamblers both with life and money, especially so if the third finger appears longer than the first.

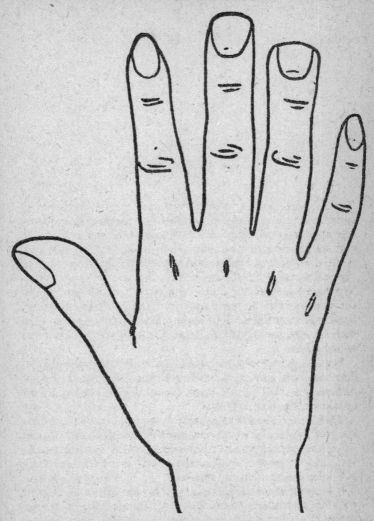

FIG. 7. THE MIXED HAND

The fingers of the hand may be either long or short irrespective of the length of the palm to which they belong.

Long fingers indicate a higher development of the mentality than when they are short. They give more love of detail in everything the mind is engaged in.

Short fingers miss the little things in both life and study. They are less thoughtful and thorough in all their undertakings. When thick, clumsy and coarse in appearance, they have less refinement and indicate that the person is closer to the brute creation.

An example of this may be taken from the monkey. The palm is longer and more developed than in the case of a man.

When the fingers are found curved inwards and stiff or apparently contracted, the mind is also contracted and more or less cautious and even timid.

If the fingers are the reverse of this, the man or woman is more open-minded, and the brain quicker in coming to conclusions and less conservative.

The extreme of this is when the fingers are so supple and loose-jointed that they can be bent over almost to the back of the hand. Such persons are too 'open-minded' for their own good. They jump to conclusions too rapidly—they change from one thing to another, and are not retentive in memorising.

Stiff fingers on the contrary are slower in absorbing knowledge. They grasp it more and hold tenaciously what they have learned.

Crooked, twisted or distorted-looking fingers—if not produced by illness—are not favourable. They denote some 'twist'

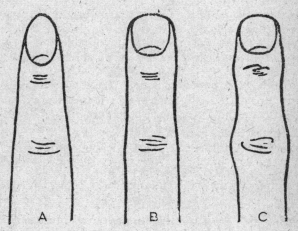

FIG. 8. THE FINGERS AND JOINTS

Pointed with smooth          Square with smooth          Square with
joints                              joints                      developed joints

as it were in the particular qualities shown by the finger that is deformed.

If the first finger appears bent towards the second, the ambitions will be more saturnine and morbid, also more hidden or concealed. The second and third fingers bent together or extremely close at the end indicate a very secretive nature.

When the fourth or little finger is crooked or bent inwards towards the third, the person is inclined to be shrewd and cunning in business or money matters, if the fourth finger is exceptionally long and if the Head Line is slightly curved upwards.

This side of the hand and 'little finger' in symbolism is the 'croupier's rake'. It means that if this part of the hand is accentuated by the fourth finger being long, the person has the nature to 'rake' things unto himself, or he has the acquisitive faculty strongly in evidence.

On the inside tip of the fingers a slight ball or pad denotes that the person is extremely sensitive or delicate in his touch, also that he feels things acutely through the mind. Such subjects can sense their way in the dark and find objects easily by touch.

When the fingers are found very full at their bases next the palm, puffy and fat-looking, the men or women demand luxury in eating, drinking and living. On the contrary if the bases of the fingers are slender with a hollow space between them, it denotes fastidiousness in regard to food or eating in general.

When the hand is stretched open and a wider space is seen between the first and second fingers than between the others, it is a distinct indication of independence of thought. When the space is wide between the third and fourth, independence of action.

### The length of the fingers to one another

When the first finger is very long the person will be ambitious to rule and have authority over others. Such a nature will 'lay down the law'. With a good Head Line it is an excellent indication. With a short first finger the person has less desire for power over others and will be inclined to be lenient and easy-going with servants and employees.

If the first finger is abnormally long equal to the second, pride of power and domination will be excessive. The great Napoleon was an example of this. On both his hands the end of the first finger came almost level with that of the second.

When the second finger (the finger of Saturn) looks heavy and especially if taking after the square type, the nature will be thoughtful, serious, introspective and of a morbid turn of mind. If rather pointed, the tendencies will be the reverse.

When the third finger (that of the Sun) is long, namely higher than the first, it shows that the desire for glory or publicity dominates the life, but with good Lines of Head and Sun it is an excellent sign on the hands of artists, or all those who follow a public career in any form.

If this finger is exceptionally long, equal to the second, the nature will be inclined to gamble with everything and go to an extreme in taking risks and chances.

A spatulate termination of the third finger, if it is not too long, is an excellent indication on the hands of public speakers or actors, as it increases their dramatic or sensational appeal to an audience.

When the fourth or little finger looks well shaped and long, it balances the hand as it were and gives mental force. If very long, almost reaching to the base of the nail on the third, it denotes power of eloquence, flow and mastery of language in speech. Gladstone's hand is a good example of this. In his case the end of the fourth or 'little' finger almost reached the nail of the third (see Gladstone's Hand, Part III).

## Smooth or jointed fingers

The joints are, figuratively speaking, walls between the phalanges of the fingers (Fig. 8). They seem to arrest or stop impulsive action. For this reason a person with a jointed formation will be more reflective and slower in coming to conclusions than the person with smooth joints.

Square fingers with the smooth formation are excellent indications in themselves, as they have the reflective, serious qualities of their class as a balance to the impulsiveness of the smooth formation.

Fingers very pointed from base to tip belong to the unreflective type of mind and act on impulse.

In any serious and scientific study of the hand, the thumb calls for special attention. It is in every sense the most important member of the hand. In every phase of humanity, the thumb has played an important rule.

In Oriental countries if prisoners beg for mercy, they close their thumb inside the fingers. In this dumb but eloquent way they indicate the *surrender of their will*.

In religion the thumb has a very deep significance. In both Protestant and Catholic churches, the blessing is given by the thumb and the two first fingers—the thumb representing God, the first finger Christ or the indicator of the will of God and the second representing the Holy Spirit as the attendant to the first.

In the Greek Church the Bishop alone makes the sign of the blessing by the thumb and the first and second fingers representing in this way the Trinity, while the ordinary priest in this Church uses the whole hand.

In the old ritual of the English Church, it is laid down that 'in baptism the cross must be made by the thumb'.

In medical science there are many proofs of the importance of the thumb, but the most striking of all is what is known as the 'thumb-centre' of the brain.

It is well known to nerve specialists that by an examination of the thumb, they can tell whether the patient is likely to be affected by paralysis or not, as the thumb indicates such a tendency a long time in advance of the slightest trace of such a thing in any other part of the system.

From the knowledge derived in this way, an operation on the thumb-centre in the brain can be performed, which, if successful (this again being shown by the thumb), will save the patient from the threatened paralysis.

Dr. Francis Galton was one of the first to demonstrate to the heads of the London police of Scotland Yard with what marvellous accuracy criminals could be traced by the whorls and corrugations on the skin of the thumb and fingers.

The police of all countries could get still more helpful information of the mental bent of criminals from an examination or impression of the entire hand. When, however, I demonstrated this to Sir Howard Vincent, the head of Scotland Yard, he answered that prejudice against the study of the hand was still too strong to allow such an experiment to be made, and he laughingly added: 'My dear sir, you would turn the entire police force into Palmists if you carried out such a plan.'

If any one of my readers cares to visit the asylums for the insane in any country, he or she cannot help but notice that without an exception all congenital idiots have weak malformed thumbs. In fact in many cases the thumbs are not properly developed even in shape.

Midwives notice the thumbs when children are born. If the child some days after birth keeps the thumb inside the palms covered by the fingers, it will to her mind be delicate in its early years. But if after seven days from the birth the thumb remains covered, she will have good reason to suspect that the child will be delicate mentally.

When a person is close to death the thumb loses its power and falls in on the hand, an indication that the will-power has given up the fight.

On the hand of a chimpanzee, the nearest approach to a human being, the thumb is small and badly formed, its tip or nail phalange barely reaching to the base of the first finger.

In the southern part of China, many natives may be found with 'double thumbs' This peculiarity is rarely met with in other races. In every case as far as I know of, the possessors of the 'double thumb' developed criminal propensities which brought them into conflict with the law.

Speaking of murderous tendencies shown on the Line of Head earlier in this book, I have alluded to the 'clubbed thumb' as usually found on the hands of those who commit murder in a moment of ungovernable passion (A, Fig. 9). If the joint of the top or nail phalange be found stiff, that is will not bend back, the temper of the person will be less controllable. A pliable or bendable thumb will be a redeeming feature in such a case

### The supple-jointed thumb

The nail phalange of the thumb if flat, slight and well formed, denotes that the temper of the man or woman is refined and gentle.

If we add to this pliability of the first phalange, the man or woman will yield to almost everything before he or she will give way to uncontrollable temper (B, Fig. 9).

A man or woman with the pliable thumb detests having 'scenes', while a person with the joint of the first phalange stiff will more or less provoke them.

Persons with the supple-jointed thumb are broadminded and liberal in their views. They are inclined to be extravagant and wasteful in money matters, but are generous in thought and action. They allow themselves to be easily imposed on, but that is largely due to the fact that they hate to quarrel, or resist any call made upon them. Also they are more inclined to promise to do things than persons with the stiff-jointed thumb.

Perhaps it is for this reason they are not 'strait-laced' or bound by conventionality. As a rule they are not as highly moral as those of the stiff thumb variety, as with their extreme broad-mindedness they easily find excuses for others as well as for themselves.

These 'bendable' thumbs are adaptable to people and

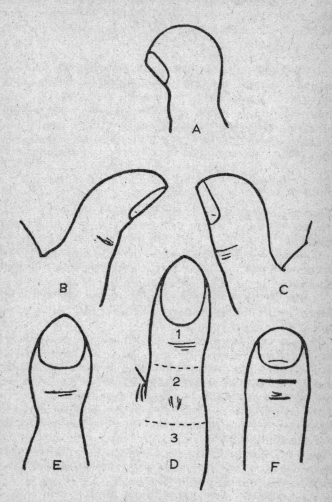

FIG. 9. THE THUMB

circumstances. They can get on with anyone and settle down easily to new work or new surroundings. They make a home quickly in whatever country they find themselves in.

### The firm-jointed thumb

Exactly the opposite qualities of the preceding are found in persons who have the firm-jointed thumb (C, Fig. 9). With the firm joint persons are less adaptable to circumstance or to people. They are more reserved, more cautious, more secretive, more conservative in every way.

They carry out their purpose with more obstinacy of will. They control self, and if they can, they also control others with a rod of iron. In other words they are as 'unbendable' in disposition as the supple-jointed thumb person is 'bendable'

### The first or nail phalange

When the first or nail phalange of the thumb is long and well formed (D, Fig. 9), it denotes a higher class of intellectual breeding than when this phalange appears coarse and brutal looking.

The shorter this nail phalange is, the less the control the person has over himself.

### The second or middle phalange

The second phalange of the thumb (D, Fig. 9) is a very important indicator of temperament and character. It has two very decided formations.

1. The moulded or waist-like appearance (E, Fig. 9).
2. The phalange full, keeping the same shape all through the second part (F, Fig. 9).

The first class being a finer formation, the person is more subtle in his reasoning ability. He has greater tact and diplomacy in dealing with other persons.

The second class, namely with this phalange full, is more forceful and tactless in his expressions. He is more brutally frank in argument and more impatient in the handling of others.

## The third phalange

The third phalange of the thumb (D, Fig. 9 is the bony structure lying by the side of the Mount of Venus. The *longer* this is, the more the man or woman has control of the sensual side of the nature. If on forcing the hand fully open this phalange appears to make the palm contracted or narrow, the man or woman is more timid in driving himself or herself out into the world. He or she will love home life and a quiet peaceful existence.

Almost from time immemorial the thumb has been divided into three sections significant of the three powers that rule the world: love, logic and will.

The first or nail phalange denotes—will.

The second—logic or reason.

The third—passionate love.

The palm of the hand when firm and elastic to the touch denotes a buoyant disposition and a healthy constitution.

A palm hard and dry as if carved of wood, with no elasticity in it, denotes a nervous worrying nature non-magnetic to others.

A soft flabby palm denotes a love of luxury and indolence with a strong undertone of sensuality.

A 'hollow palm', especially if at the same time hard, is an unfortunate indication. There is just a hidden something about such a person that generally attracts ill-luck and disappointment

## Large and small hands

It may appear difficult to believe, and yet it is the case as anyone can prove for himself, that persons with very large hands do the finest work, especially in the execution of detail with precision. Such hands are always found among diamond setters, engravers, etchers, watch makers and suchlike trades, but in every case the fingers are long. The very handwriting of persons with large hands is as a rule small and fine.

Small hands on the contrary go in for large ideas. They generally detest detail of all kinds and their writing is usually large and bold.

It is quite probable that many of my readers have never taken the trouble to notice the difference in the shape of the nails on their finger-tips from those of their friends.

If they had they would be astonished to find that there are hardly two persons who have nails alike.

After reading this book they will, I hope, begin to observe what a wealth of information can be gained from a study of their own nails and those of others.

To begin with, a study of the nails is most important as regards health and disease. They are remarkably sure indications to go by. Whether they care to admit it or not, nearly all doctors quietly observe the nails of the patient they are examining. They know the nails give hereditary indications of symptoms which may not be manifested by other parts of the body.

The nails not only disclose secrets relating to health, but they also give information about the temperament or disposition.

It must be borne in mind that care of the nails does not affect the type they belong to in the slightest degree. Whether they are broken by work or polished with care—*the type remains unchanged.*

Nails are divided into four classes, long, short, broad and narrow.

## Long nails

Very long, or, as they are called, filbert-shaped nails, never indicate such physical strength as short or broad ones.

Long nails are called filbert-shaped because they have the appearance of filbert nuts (D and E, Fig. 10).

The long nail tells of some tendency (generally inherited) for delicacy of the lungs.

Very long and very pale in colour they indicate a consumptive tendency. This is still more accentuated if they should be bluish in colour, and have marks like ribs rising up from one end to the other (E, Fig. 10).

The same type of nail, but slightly shorter, indicates bronchial tendencies. Long nails extremely narrow show spinal weakness and general delicacy of the entire system (F, Fig. 10).

## Short nails

Short round-shaped nails show danger of trouble with the throat and passage of the nose. Illnesses such as asthma, laryngitis, bronchitis, etc., are always associated with this particular type of short nail (A, B, C, Fig. 10).

Short nails, thin and very flat at their base, with little or no moons are indicative of weak action of the heart, poor circulation and heart disease (G, H and I, Fig. 10).

Large moons on any type of nail promise good circulation of the blood and a strong heart action. The normal pulse of such persons will be found to be more rapid than those who have little or no moons.

When the nails appear very flat and sunken into the flesh, especially if ribbed, they threaten nerve diseases of one form or another.

If very flat and shell-shaped (J, K and L, Fig. 10), they indicate a danger of paralysis. This danger will be still more

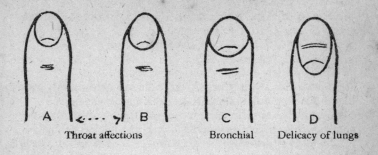

Throat affections      Bronchial   Delicacy of lungs

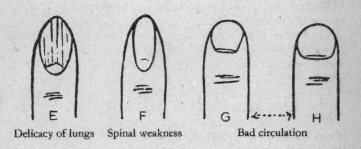

Delicacy of lungs  Spinal weakness     Bad circulation

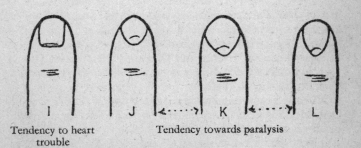

Tendency to heart     Tendency towards paralysis
    trouble

FIG. 10. THE NAILS

accentuated if at the same time such nails are white and brittle and inclined to lift up at the edges.

White spots like flecks on the nails denote an over-strong nervous temperament, and danger of nervous prostration, especially if there are no moons or very small ones.

Lines or ribs across the nails from side to side show recent illness (D, Fig. 10). As nails take nine months to grow from the base to the outer edge, a heavy rib in the structure of the nails about their centre would indicate that between four and five months previously the breakdown or illness had taken place and so had arrested the growth of the nail.

Very thin nails inclined to split or break easily denote delicate health.

When the nail phalange of each finger has a ball-like appearance with round-looking nails without moons, an aggravated form of heart-disease may be expected. An example of this may be seen by the impression of a boy's hand (Plate 2).

He had malformation of the heart from birth. When I took the impression of his hand he was seven years of age. Medical science had kept him alive till then. He died later in his tenth year.

This impression is useful as an example of the ball-like formation of the ends of the fingers. The nails were completely round in shape—very blue in colour and without the slightest sign of any moons.

## Disposition as shown by the nails

People with long filbert nails are more placid and calm in temper than those with short nails. They have a great deal of ideality for the reason that for long nails the end phalange must also be long. As a rule this type of nail denotes the artistic visionary disposition, whereas short nails belong to the critical type of person, as if the short tips of the fingers were made to pick things up and examine them more closely.

Short-nailed persons are more analytical, even of themselves and their own work. They always incline to logic and reason in direct opposition to the more visionary qualities of those who have the long type.

They are good in debate, keen and sharp in their arguments and quick to make their points. They are more easily roused in temper than those who have long nails.

When the nails are more broad than long they indicate a quarrelsome, irritable disposition, one inclined to take offence at little things.

Indications of health as shown by the nails should be judged with the appearance of the Lines of Head and Life as I shall explain when dealing with those lines in relation to illness or disease.

*Part 2*  Cheiromancy

## Chapter 13 The difference between the right and left hands

The first principle I use in the reading of hands is that the left 'is the hand you are born with—the right is the hand you make'. The most casual observer is at once struck with the difference seen between the lines of the left and right hands. I therefore advocate that at the commencement of reading, both the left and right should be closely examined together.

If there is very little variation in the lines of the two hands, one may safely conclude that the subject has led a vegetable life and practically remained as he was born. The most important line to notice for changes will naturally be that of the Line of Head. On the left hand it may slope towards the Mount of Luna, indicating an imaginative and dreamy nature, whereas on the right hand it may have become perfectly straight. This will at once indicate that the practical side of the nature has been developed, and the inherited tendencies, artistic or imaginative, deliberately laid aside.

On the other hand, the change may be seen in the opposite direction—namely that the Line of Head on the right hand has sloped towards the Mount of Luna whereas on the left it is marked as perfectly straight. The reverse has therefore taken place, and it often indicates that the subject being born with a practical trend may have been engaged in business or commerce for some years and later in life developed imagination or artistic tendencies.

This is very often seen in the case of a writer or artist who has deliberately broken away from the tradition or conventions of his family.

Changes may, of course, be seen in all the other lines in the hand, the meaning of the difference in every case being that the indications shown on the right hand are produced by developments and alterations from the characteristics and circumstances shown by the left.

It is quite usual to find the Line of Fate looking as if it were tied down to the Life Line on the left hand—whereas on the right it may stand out boldly from the Life Line with a space as big as a quarter to half an inch between the lines. The inference to be drawn is that the subject had been greatly hampered by home circumstances, or people binding him through love and affection in the early years, and that he had, by developing great independence of character, broken free from such conditions.

In reference to health, the comparison of the two hands is most important. For instance, one may show a very poor, badly formed line of life in the left hand, and a strong, powerful-looking line in the right. One can then say with absolute authority that in the early years bad health and great delicacy had been present, whereas by the life led in later years robust vitality and strong constitution had been developed.

When the Life Line is found broken in both hands, it is usually a distinct sign that the life will not be long, and where the break is found in both hands would be the threatened point of death. Should, however, the break be found on the left and not on the right, the inference then is that at the date where the break is marked on the left hand there is likelihood of serious illness from which—according to the date of reading—the person has or will completely recover, averting the danger of death.

As I will go into all these questions later in great detail line by line, I will conclude by the simple statement that the left hand shows the hereditary or inherited qualities, whereas the right shows the developed talents or tendencies, or those that will be developed as the life goes on.

In consequence of this interesting characteristic of scientific palmistry, the future cannot be foretold from the lines in the left hand, as curiously enough lines indicating events are quite likely to appear in the left hand *after their passage*, whereas the right hand may show such things many years in advance.

It is a well known medical fact that the average human being uses the left side of the brain, and that the nerves cross and go to the right side of the body—consequently the right hand shows the faculties in use and those in process of development.

The old practice of reading the left hand because it was 'nearest the heart' belonged to the many superstitions which degraded this science in the Middle Ages. But even today there are some so-called palmists who may be found still clinging to the old superstitions.

In order to make the study as easy and interesting as possible, I strongly recommend students to work from impressions of hands rather than the hands themselves. The impressions can easily be taken by the student. He should obtain a small gelatine roller, and a tube of fingerprint ink, together with a quantity of smooth white paper with no watermark, as this will show through the hand print.

Roll a small quantity of the ink evenly on to the inside of the hand from wrist to finger-tips and over the thumb.* Immediately press the hand down firmly on to a sheet of the paper, making sure to obtain a clear, unsmudged impression.

Surgical spirit applied on cotton wool is excellent for removing the ink from the hands after the impressions have been made. There are many preparations suitable for this purpose which can be bought at any chemist, general store or garage.

The student should collect as many hand prints as possible to assist him in his studies.

---

* It would be better first to squeeze a little of the ink on to a piece of thick glass or a square of Formica, running the roller over it until evenly coated, then transfer the ink on the roller to the inside of the hand.—L.O.

*Chapter 14*  Cheiromancy—the meaning of the lines on the hand

The word Cheiromancy is derived from the Greek word *Cheir*—the hand. From this Greek word I originated the name 'Cheiro' as my *nom de guerre* or professional name, under which I have practised since I wrote my first treatise on the lines of the hand when I was twelve years of age.

The year before I reached my twelfth birthday, my mother, who was herself of Greek descent, taught me the meaning of the shapes of hands and what their lines indicated and handed over to me the considerable library she had collected on the subject. She little dreamed at that early period of my life that I would eventually take up the study seriously, make of it a profession, through it meet Kings, Queens, Presidents of Republics and many other of the most distinguished men and women of the age.

She had, however, at about this time in my life jotted down in her note-book some of the salient points in my character. Among other things she wrote the following: 'My son has in his left and right hands the sign of the Mystic Cross. For this reason I have given over to him all the books of occultism I possess, and especially those on the study of the hand. I believe he will make good use of these books. Even now in his early years I have noticed how he studies such works more than all

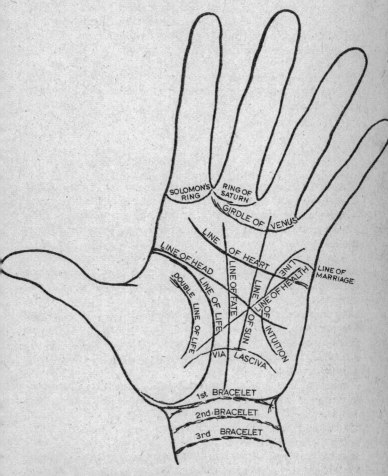

FIG. 11. MAP OF THE HAND

others. He is certain to become a writer, and will, from what I foresee in his hand, make a name for himself in connection with these subjects.'

My mother was right in her judgment. From that time onwards I spent all my spare time looking at hands, and my spare cash on buying books on occult subjects, and so these studies became the ruling passion of my life.

We will now consider the lines in the hand and I will endeavour to put whatever knowledge I have gained from study, investigation and long professional experience at the disposal of my readers.

## *The Line of Head*

The Line of Head (see map of the hand) relates to everything that concerns mentality. Such things as education, improvement of the mind—its outlook on life, morals and its mental attitude towards others.

It indicates—and with unfailing precision—the leanings or tendencies of the brain; its inherited qualities, and those that have been developed by work, study or the vicissitudes of experience.

Like the needle of a compass it points straight across the palm, or downwards or upwards as the case may be, each and every deviation having its definite and distinct meaning.

Further it shows the character and even quality of the brain it represents. It shows in advance—*often many years in advance*—that 'undermining something' that like a canker is already eating the tissues or brain cells, and preparing the way for the inevitable mental breakdown.

I will illustrate these points in the chapter dealing with the Line of Head itself.

## *The Line of Heart*

The Line of Heart, as indicated by the name given to it, relates to the affections rather than to the sensual or passionate side of the nature with which it is often confused.

## The Line of Fate or Destiny

The Line of Fate or Destiny might be better understood were it considered the Line of Individuality or Personality.

The hidden God-essence of the man or woman, as it fights the battle—not of fate, but with fate—is indicated by this line. By its strength or weakness can be determined how the battle has gone, the 'broken bridges' it has crossed, or whether the individuality has become submerged by the floods of 'outrageous fortune'.

Again it shows the character of the individual—the 'I am' of the soul that urges it onward.

Some hands have strongly marked Lines of Fate, which do not, however, attract other lines to them. In such cases the individuality may be strong, but it is more or less lonely or isolated, and may produce less effect than a more finely traced Fate Line with 'influence lines' or 'attendant lines' travelling as it were by its side.

Next in position running up the centre of the palm to, or towards, the base of the third finger, must be considered a still more mysterious line.

## The Line of Sun or Success

As the Sun is to the Earth, giving fertility, wealth and happiness, so this line is to the hand, or more especially so to the Line of Fate or Individuality.

It is the most mysterious of all the signs. From the date at which it appears, especially if coming from the Fate Line, success in some form or another is usually a certainty. The nature of the success is estimated by the kind of hand on which it is found. A successful preacher may have this mark, so may a successful criminal for that matter.

This line, like the Sun it stands for, brings fruition to the purpose and ambitions of the individual.

It may bring publicity and glory to an actress or a film star. It is likely to be the turning-point towards fame. To a painter his first picture recognised. To a writer a first book accepted, but to one and all it is a marked period in the destiny—a milestone, white, red, or black, as the case may be.

## The Line of Life

The Line of Life is that line traced round what is called the ball of the thumb. By its position, depth, freedom from breaks, islands, length, etc., may be judged the general health, constitution, and duration of life that may be expected.

## The Line of Health

The Line of Health was in more ancient times also called the Hepatica. Again it has been called the 'Liver Line' because in those days almost all ailments were put down to disorders of the liver. This line descends down the hand from underneath the fourth finger, otherwise called the Finger of Mercury.

Mercury represents the mind, and so worry and mental anxiety will often cause this line to deepen or to lessen according to the mental strain the person goes through. It is excellent if the line is missing from the hand, as its presence shows some unusual wear and tear on the mental machinery that is undermining the vital forces. When extremely strong in the early part, namely from the Mount of Mercury, to the end of the Line of Head, it denotes a tendency for nervous breakdown in the early years. Children with this mark heavily indicated should be spared in every way from mental work in their school routine. They should be made to rest as much as possible lest the anxiety over their examinations completely undermines their health.

As a rule, however, it is more marked in hands later on in life, and may be found increasing in strength from the Head Line downwards until it cuts or injures the Line of Life.

Where these two lines meet is always a danger spot in the years indicated, and if the Health Line appears stronger than the Life Line at the point of impact, it is invariably the sign of breakdown and death.

### The Line of Marriage

The Line of Marriage is generally considered as the line (or lines) found across the face of the Mount of Mercury at the base of the fourth finger. There are, however, other indications of love and marriage which I will explain fully when I come to the chapter dealing with this subject.

## MINOR LINES OF THE HAND

### The Line of Mars

The Line of Mars, or, as it is otherwise known, the Inner Vital or Double Life Line, as a rule rises on the Mount of Mars itself and runs down by the side of the Line of Life. It is generally a strongly marked line and cannot be confused with what are called Influence Lines on the Mount of Venus.

The Line of Mars denotes excess of health, especially on all square or broad hands, and on such types it usually adds to the nature a rather quarrelsome fighting disposition, as well as robust strength. It is an excellent mark to be found on the hands of soldiers or fighters of all kinds.

If found by a delicate-looking Line of Life on a long narrow hand, it appears to support the life, and often carries it past any dangerous breaks or signs of illness as it adds vitality to the constitution.

### The Girdle of Venus

The Girdle of Venus is that broken or unbroken kind of semi-circle often found lying from the base of the first and second fingers and finishing between the third and fourth. As a rule this line is associated with highly sensitive intellectual natures. It has a peculiar relation to the love nature, because it usually increases the mental desire for love and affection. People possessing this mark are usually enthusiastic over anything that engages their fancy, but they are people of mercurial moods—one moment in the highest spirits, the next despondent and gloomy.

When the Girdle of Venus goes over the outer side of the hand and comes in contact with the Line of Marriage, the happiness of the marriage will be interfered with on account of the peculiarities of the mental moods and temperamental vagaries of the subject.

## The Ring of Saturn

The Ring of Saturn is very seldom found. It is not a good sign to possess. It appears to cut off the successful ending of the Line of Destiny. It also appears to accentuate the Saturnian nature, and with a very sloping Line of Head exaggerates the tendencies towards suicide.

## The bracelets

The bracelets are not of much importance in relation to character or in the study of the hand itself. There is one point, however, that has a curious medical significance as it relates to weakness or some curious formation in the lower organs of the body. A bracelet arching into the base of a palm on a woman's hand foreshadows long, protracted child-birth and danger from such causes.

If, however, the bracelets are well formed, especially the top one nearest the palm, they increase the promise of sound health and robust constitution.

## The Via Lasciva

The Via Lasciva is often confused with the Health Line. It is, however, totally distinct, both in its markings and its meaning. It is in reality a kind of loop line joining the base of the Mount of Luna with that of Venus. Its meaning is that it gives lascivious ideas, which by working on the mind generally shorten the natural length of life by its excesses, and if accompanied by

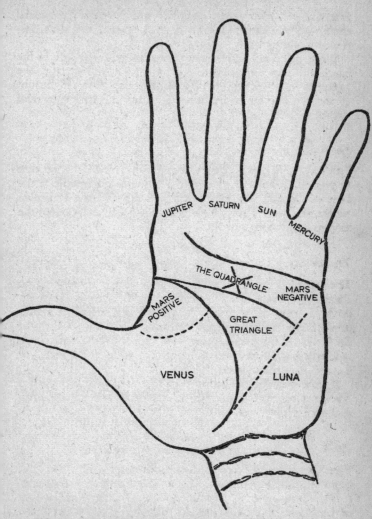

JUPITER  SATURN  SUN  MERCURY

THE QUADRANGLE

MARS
POSITIVE

MARS
NEGATIVE

GREAT
TRIANGLE

VENUS  LUNA

FIG. 12. THE MOUNTS, THE QUADRANGLE, THE GREAT TRIANGLE
AND MYSTIC CROSS

the Girdle of Venus, especially on a soft hand, it is as a rule a most sinister mark to possess.

### The Line of Intuition

The Line of Intuition is more often found on the Philosophic, the Conic, and the Psychic than on any other of the seven types of hand. Its form is that of a distant semi-circle, and is generally found from the base of the Mount of Mercury to the lower part of the Mount of Luna. It denotes a keenly sensitive person both to surroundings and influence. It gives a tendency towards all matters of intuition and presentiment, and a love of dealing with such things as clairvoyance, clairaudience, and a desire to investigate such matters as dreams, visions and spiritualism.

### The Mystic Cross

The Mystic Cross (Fig. 12) is found in the centre of the Quadrangle—the space formed by the Head and Heart Lines. It is generally found directly under the Mount of Saturn. It denotes a strong leaning in the nature to mysticism, occultism and in some cases the pursuit of magic.

### The Ring of Solomon

The Ring of Solomon is usually found as a kind of semi-circle apparently joining the Mounts of Saturn and Jupiter together. This increases the power of the adept or master in all mystic pursuits. In fact it appears to intensify gifts of this nature, so that the person with this sign and that of the Mystic Cross reaches the pinnacle of authority on such subjects.

### Time as shown on the Hand

The Time Factor in the Hand (see Figs. 59 and 60) illustrating dates is clearly indicated. Dates and periods of time are important in the forecasting of events. The centre of the hand is taken as the centre of the normal span of life   an average of seventy years, making the centre of the palm indicate the age of thirty-five. On normal hands as a rule the meeting-point of the Line of Fate and the Line of Head takes this central position, and an event indicated in this crossing can be taken as on or about thirty-five years of age. This is fully dealt with in a special chapter on Time and Dates of Events to be found later on in this book.

# *Chapter 15* The Line of the Head

The Line of the Head (Map of the Hand) is the most important line in the reading of the hand. It has so many variations, both in the positions it takes on the hand, and in the meaning it gives to innumerable traits of character, that for the benefit of the student I will describe this line in sections.

## *The type of hand*

This must be the first consideration in reading the meaning of the Line of Head. For example, a sloping Line of Head on a psychic or conic hand would not be of such importance as if the same sloping Line of Head were found on a square hand. The reason for this is the following:

The sloping line or one bending downwards to the Mount of Luna is more natural on the philosophic, psychic or conic hands, whereas on a square hand it is in opposition to the qualities expressed by the square type. I must here digress to speak of the types of the hand, especially in relation to the Line of Head.

The square hand (see chapter on Shapes of Hands) being the foundation of what might be called a 'squareheaded' person, or one whose natural inclination is to be thoroughly level-headed and practical, is normally found with the Line of Head lying straight across the palm. The sloping Line of Head on such a type would therefore be a contradiction.

Consequently, when the Line of Head appears to bend downwards towards the Mount of Luna, one gets a tendency for imagination and invention. These qualities in turn governed by the nature of the square hand are likely to manifest themselves in practical inventions of material value to the world at large.

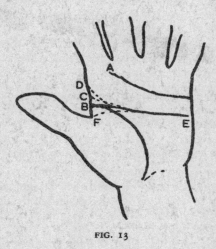

FIG. 13

On a psychic, conic or philosophic type it would be more inclined to make itself manifest in dreams of the imagination, or in a mentality more visionary than practical. It would therefore be more associated with painters, writers and others who specialise in abstract works of imagination.

Imagination manifests itself in many forms—art, invention, science, politics, social work—therefore the type of imagination is determined by the type of hand on which the sloping Head Line appears.

*Position of the line*

The Head Line has a normal place in the palm as the nose has a normal place on the face, therefore any abnormality in position indicates an abnormal mental tendency.

The beginning of the Line of Head is found under the first finger, or joined with the Line of Life at its commencement. There are three distinct positions from which the Line of Head may take its source.

1. Inside the Line of Life on the Mount of Mars.
2. Where the Line of Life and the Line of Head are closely joined together.
3. The Line of Head standing out independently of the Line of Life, and leaving a space large or small, as the case may be, between these two main lines.

These three are normal manifestations of the Line of Head.

*The first position of the source*

Rising on the Mount of Mars the Head Line appears to carry with it the qualities designated by the planet Mars. It would indicate a tendency to argumentative fighting and a more or less quarrelsome disposition, which will be intensified if the Line of Head runs straight across the hand in the direction of what is called the Mount of Mars negative on the opposite side (F to E, Fig. 13).

Should this particular Line of Head turn upwards even slightly at its farthest end, rising as it were towards or against the Line of Heart, there is the indication of a quarrelsome, irritable individual with more or less murderous instincts (B, Fig. 14).

If the Line of Head turns downwards towards the Mount of Luna, the quarrelsome disposition is more or less softened by introspection (C, Fig. 14).

*The second position of the source*

The Line of Head which is joined to the Line of Life at its

source indicates an extremely sensitive, and more or less over-cautious person. Also an individual who lacks self-confidence in expressing his views and carrying out his ideas. Even very clever people with an exceptionally good Line of Head are hampered by the qualities expressed by this junction with the Line of Life (B, Fig. 13).

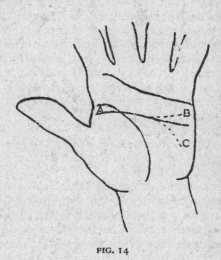

FIG. 14

### The third position of the source

When the Line of Head is independent of the Line of Life with a slight space between, and the line goes well across the hand, the space denotes strong independence of mentality. It is the sign of an independent thinker. One who is rarely bound down by conventionality, who is not hampered by too much caution, and who has as a rule sufficient self-confidence to stand up and express his views (C, Fig. 13).

It is for this reason that people with the open space between the Lines of Head and Life drift more easily into public life. They can more readily express their ideas. They have considerable command of language, and what might be described as the 'call of the public' seems to be one of the impelling motives of their lives. This mark in moderation is a successful sign. Consequently if found on the hands of preachers, actors, politicians and in fact all those whose activities bring them before the public, it indicates particular suitability for their chosen work.

An exceptionally fine modification is when the Line of Head rises high on the Mount of Jupiter, and in descending touches or is slightly connected with the Line of Life. This gives such a marvellous quality of independence of mind and yet prudence, that it is one of the most successful indications to possess (D, Fig. 13).

### The first position of the termination

As there are three normal positions for the Line of Head to rise, so there are three normal positions for it to terminate at the opposite side of the hand.

The first is that of a perfectly straight Line of Head (E, Fig. 13), that might have been drawn by a ruler from one side to the other. This indicates an extremely practical person, one of sound judgment and 'level-headed' ability. It is also indicative of great organising ability in whatever sphere of life it functions.

A woman having this Head Line on the square or practical type of hand can be expected to manifest almost masculine qualities in her gifts of organisation, business acumen and industrial control.

### The second position of the termination

This is where the end of the Head Line is bent slightly upwards, or sends a branch line in an upward direction. On a long clear line it is also an indication of strong mental power, but one of a more grasping or acquisitive nature. It is a magnificent sign on the hands of all those who make wealth their idol (A, Fig. 15).

### The third position of the termination

This is where the Line of Head slopes slightly downwards. This gives the blend of the practical with the artistic, and is often found as an apparent contradiction in the hands of

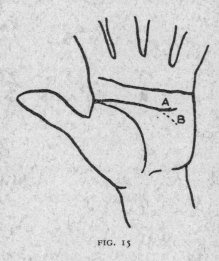

FIG. 15

business people. Such people will work hard all day at their commercial occupations and relieve their tension by following some artistic pursuit in their homes (B, Fig. 15).

### The course of the line

The Line of Head may cross the hand in a straight line as if drawn by a ruler, or it may rise and fall in its centre or show a deep depression. This affects the shape and size of the space between the Line of Heart and Line of Head known as the Quadrangle. The Quadrangle (Fig. 12) has an important bearing on the reading of the hand, and will be dealt with later by itself.

*Marks on the Line of Head*

The most important marks on the Line of Head are islands. Islands mark a complete or partial breakdown of the mental powers while the island lasts. The nature of the breakdown is indicated by the position of the island on the line. There are four possible positions which are governed by the mounts, and tracing the origin to its source, by the respective planets.

For example, an island under the Mount of Jupiter (under 1st finger, Fig. 16), will indicate a breakdown caused by excessive ambition. Under Saturn (under 2nd finger, Fig. 16), a breakdown due to the development of the more morbid and introspective qualities. Under the Mount of the Sun (3rd finger, Fig. 16), overwork in connection with the achievement of fame or success. Under Mercury, mental strain through worry connected with business, commerce or research in the pursuit of science (Fig. 16).

In the case of the islands in the Line of Head read the nature from the position, and look for the time of the breakdowns in confirming breaks or weaknesses in the Lines of Health and Life.

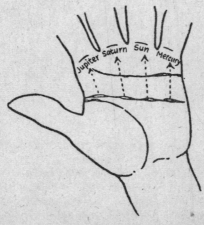

FIG. 16

When a distinct island is seen in the Line of Head in a child's hand, it gives a distinct warning that the child should be carefully guarded against anxiety and mental strain in order to strengthen the brain for later years. Such vigilance will probably be rewarded by the fading or disappearance of the island.

These islands should not be confused with the Chain Formation of the Line of Head, which may exist either in part or in its entire length (A, Fig. 17). This indicates a brain of extreme delicacy which is not strong enough to be subjected to mental strain, worry or responsibility. Where the line commences with a chain and becomes clear and definite towards the end, it indicates strengthening and recovery as the life goes on, but where the line begins clear and straight and develops into a chain, it indicates delicacy appearing towards the middle or end of life.

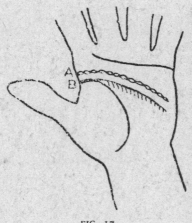

FIG. 17

When the Line of Head is composed of a series of tiny lines instead of one clear unbroken line, it indicates a tendency to mental paralysis (B, Fig. 17). The brain works intermittently. If one sees such an example it is advisable to recommend a quiet life without work, responsibility or excitement. Like the previous example of the chained Head Line, this hair-like formation may be found in any part of the Line of Head.

If dents or little holes appear in the line itself on pressing the Line of Head, they indicate a tendency to a series of accidents to the head. Signs of this nature are rarely seen unless you press the line in order to examine it closely.

Other marks that may be found on the Line of Head are a sign like a square, a circle, or a triangle or a star. The square is a sign of preservation wherever found. The star is a sign of temporary excess of mental effort or increase of mental power. The circle and triangle are similar in nature to the square, but they are more or less signs of protection, especially when found on the Line of Head.

### Breaks in the Line of Head

What are called 'breaks' in the Line of Head may be found in any portion of the line (A, Fig. 18). They do not always mean accidents, but they generally indicate some misfortune by which the person's head is injured. If the Line of Fate is found running into one of these 'breaks' in the Head Line, it gener-

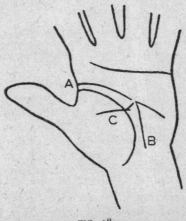

FIG 18

ally indicates injury to the head itself, and death if the main lines of Fate and Head seem to clash (B, Fig. 18). Such an indication may or may not be further confirmed by the Line of Life being short, having a break in it, or an island or a line cutting through it like a bar, which would by its position on the line give the date of death (C, Fig. 18).

A good illustration of this can be seen in the hand of Major John A. Logan (Plate 3). At exactly thirty-five years of age Major Logan was shot through the head and killed while leading his regiment into action at the Battle of Santiago, Cuba, in the Spanish-American war.

I predicted to Major Logan that he would lose his life by an accident to his head many years before there were indications of a war. A fine horseman and very fond of riding, he naturally anticipated danger from a fall from his horse. A year before the war he sold his stable and said to his friends, 'I am determined to baffle Cheiro's prediction. I won't ride a horse till after my thirty-fifth year.' Unfortunately for him the war broke out a year later and he was killed in action exactly a month past his thirty-fifth year.

These breaks indicating fatalities or tragedies are usually found more or less under the Mount of Saturn.

## Nature of the Line of Head

The main characteristics of the Line of Head to be borne in mind are shown in Fig. 19.

When this line is found straight, clear and even, it denotes practical common sense and a development of the reasoning faculties rather than the imaginative. When straight in the first half and sloping downwards in the second it shows a balance between the purely imaginative and the purely practical. Such a person would have a practical and common-sense way of going to work even when dealing with imaginative and artistic things (A, Fig. 19).

When the entire line is found with a graceful slope, especially bending like a bow towards the Mount of Luna, the drift of the nature is towards some form of imaginative work such as painting, literature or music, especially if the Mount of Luna be more or less pronounced (B, Fig. 19).

There is, however, a sloping Head Line which is indicative of danger in the form of suicidal tendencies and mental depression. The difference between the two lines is this. The imaginative line rides over the mount and slopes towards the

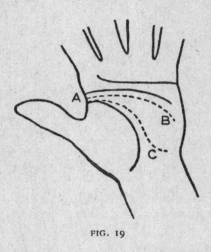

FIG. 19

side of the hand. The melancholy line bends when it reaches the mount and slopes inside as if outlining it. The latter line is an unfortunate indication of a mental inability to cope with practical matters or assume responsibility (C, Fig. 19).

A long straight Line of Head going directly from one side of the hand to the other denotes that the subject has more than usual intellectual power, and more especially so if at the source it rises independently of the Line of Life. (See impression of Gladstone's hand, Plate II.)

When the line is short, barely reaching the middle of the hand, it indicates a nature that is thoroughly materialistic. Such a man will lack all the imaginative faculties although he might be completely successful in business and industrial affairs.

## The Murderer's Mark

Before embarking on the following descriptions I must warn the student once again that one line or sign cannot be taken alone. The Head Line (as shown, Figs. 20 and 21) by itself indicates complete concentration on personal affairs to the exclusion of all other considerations, thus showing a strong tendency to be unscrupulous in achieving the object, but not necessarily to the point of violence.

A combination of the Lines of Head and Heart running across the palm in one straight line must not be confused with what is known as the 'Murderer's Mark' (A, Fig. 20).

Here it will be seen the Line of Head rises on the Mount of Mars (positive), and either cuts through the Heart Line or runs into it.

This sign is more often found on the right hand than on the left, which is only logical as it shows mental development.

Earlier in these pages I have shown that when the Line of Head even slightly curves upward at its termination, it indicates the grasping tendency of the mentality towards the acquisition and love of wealth.

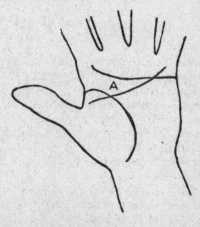

FIG. 20

In the case under examination, these propensities become abnormal, the affectionate and natural desires become subjugated or completely annihilated, the result being an absolute disregard for other human beings. The subject on whose hands this mark appears becomes obsessed with the idea of obtaining money at any cost, and will stick at nothing to gratify this desire.

In such an example murder for gain becomes a methodical study rather than the simple act of killing in a sudden outburst of passion or rage. This mark is more often found on the hands of those who use poison, or some secret means of getting rid of their victims. The Line of Head in such a case may or may not rise on the Mount of Mars.

Should it rise on Mars, the mark indicates a naturally more quarrelsome disposition than if it is simply joined to the Line of Life in the ordinary way, and the final act of murder is more likely to take place in a sudden access of hatred when a suitable opportunity offers itself.

When such a Head Line as A, Fig. 21 is found joined to the Line of Life, the person is even more deadly in his planning.

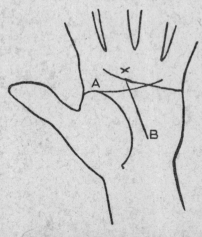

FIG. 21

He will have more caution and more patience in carrying out the crime. He will be more inclined to associate or live with his victim for years or try again and again after repeated failure to accomplish his deadly design.

In all such cases should the Line of Fate terminate at the Heart Line under either the Mount of Saturn or the Sun, it may be taken that that will be the approximate date in the career of the subject when the crime or crimes will be found out (B, Fig. 21).

A distinct cross on the Mount of Saturn either close to the end of the Fate Line or above it will emphasise still more the fatal end of the subject's murderous plans. This cross on Saturn has been called the 'mark of the scaffold', and has been found in many cases of those who have been executed for murder.

During my professional career I came across several examples of the 'Murderer's Mark'.

One instance was that of Dr. Meyer who became known as 'the Chicago poisoner'. Impressions on paper were brought to me on the occasion of my first visit to the United States by reporters of the *New York World* who wanted to test my powers.

They submitted about a dozen impressions of hands without giving the slightest clue as to whom the hands belonged to. (In all these tests I was successful in accurately describing the character and class of life each person lived.)

When I came to the impressions of Meyer's hands, I was struck by the fact that the lines on his left were normal in every way, while on the right the Head Line had risen out of its place and cut into the Line of Heart as may be seen (Plate 4). I summed up the impressions before me by stating 'the owner of these hands undoubtedly commenced his career in a normal way. He was even likely to have been a religious man in his early years.' I even ventured the idea that he might have commenced life as a Sunday School teacher. Later the desire for wealth came into his brain as distinctly shown by the upward trend of the Line of Head in the right hand.

I went on to describe how his entire nature had changed

under the continual urge to acquire riches at any cost until finally murder for money became as nothing in his eyes.

My remarks noted down by the reporters were as follows: 'Whether this man has committed one crime or twenty is not the question. As he enters his forty-fourth year he will be tried for murder and condemned to death. It will then be found that for years he has used his intelligence and whatever profession he has followed to obtain money by crime, and has stopped at nothing to achieve his ends. He will be sentenced to death, yet his hands show his life will not end in this manner. He will live for years—but in prison.'

When the interview appeared in the *New York World* it was disclosed that these hands I had read were those of Dr. Meyer. He had just been arrested in his forty-fourth year, and a few weeks later was convicted of having used his profession as a doctor to poison wealthy patients whom he had insured for considerable amounts of money.

He was sentenced to die by the electric chair. The sentence was appealed against. Three trials took place. At the third he was again condemned to death. A week before his execution he requested that I would come and see him. I was taken to his cell in Sing-Sing, New York. As long as I live I shall never forget such an interview.

'Cheiro,' gasped the now completely broken man, 'at that interview you gave the reporters, what you said about my early life was true. But you also said that although I would be sentenced to death my life would not end in that manner— that I would live for some years—but in prison. I have lost my third and last appeal—in a few days I am to be executed. For God's sake tell me if you stand by your words that I shall escape "the chair".'

Even if I had not seen his Line of Life going on clear and distinct well past his forty-fourth year, I believe I would have tried to give him some hope. Even though I could hardly believe what I saw, I pointed out that his Line of Life showed no sign of any break—so I left him, giving the hope that some miracle could still happen that would save him from the dreaded 'chair'.

Day after day went past with no news to relieve the tension. The evening papers full of details of the preparations for the execution fixed for the next morning were eagerly bought up. I bought one and read every line.

Midnight came. Suddenly boys rushed through the streets screaming 'special edition'. I read across the front page; 'Meyer escapes the "chair". Supreme Court finds flaw in indictment.' The miracle had happened—the sentence was altered to imprisonment for life. Meyer lived on for fifteen years. When the end did come he died peacefully in the prison hospital.

Murder as the outcome of a sudden fit of passion may be foreseen by the summing up of various flaws of temperament whose cumulative effect will produce the ungovernable impulse to murder.

One of these indications is what is known as the 'clubbed thumb', otherwise called the 'murderer's thumb' (A, Fig. 22). The 'clubbed thumb' is so designated from the fact that it has every appearance of being a 'club', and the curious thing about it is that those who possess it generally kill their victim by

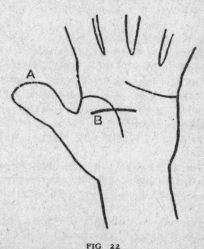

FIG 22

employing a club or some heavy article to strike the fatal blow.

The 'clubbed thumb' is in itself the signification of an animal nature. It indicates that people possessing such a formation have little or no control over themselves in a moment of rage or passion. They simply strike their enemy down when they 'see red', but once the paroxysm is over, they equally quickly regret their impetuous action.

A short thick-set Head Line from the Mount of Mars usually accompanies such a thumb (B, Fig. 22). Such a Line of Head is in itself an indication of little mental development or self-control.

One should therefore warn such a subject that it would be well to practise restraint over the temper and passion, lest they commit murder in some evil moment of rage and excitement.

Medical science teaches that there is such a thing as a 'thumb centre' in the brain. It therefore follows that some malformation of the brain may produce the 'clubbed thumb'.

As this part relates chiefly to peculiarities shown on the Line of Head, I cannot close it without reference to another formation called 'the double Line of Head' (A, Fig. 23). This mark is rarely found, but when it is, it is worthy of serious consideration.

When formed as in A, Fig. 23, the character shown by each line is in apparent contradiction to the other. For example, the lower line closely joined to the Line of Life denotes a mentality extremely sensitive, artistic and imaginative.

The upper line gives the reverse characteristics—namely, rising on the Mount of Jupiter and running nearly straight across the palm, it denotes self-confidence, ambition, power to dominate others and a level-headed practical way of looking at life.

One can hardly imagine such mentally opposite characteristics in the same person, but the impression given on Plate 5 is from my own hand and offers a good example of the 'double Line of Head'.

On the left hand there is no sign whatever of any upper Head Line—there is only the lower line to be seen, and it is a curious fact that the appearance of the upper Head Line on the right hand only commenced to be noticeable when I was about thirty years of age.

About this period of my life circumstances brought me before the world as a lecturer and public speaker. This forced me to make a supreme effort to overcome the extreme sensitiveness as shown by the lower Head Line, with the result that the upper line began to develop, and in a few years became the dominant one on my right hand.

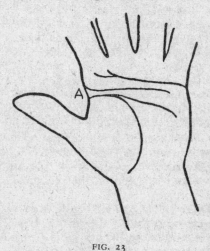

FIG. 23

As I stated in my previous work, *Language of the Hand*, a 'double Line of Head' is very rarely found, but it is an unusual sign of brain power and mentality. Such persons have great versatility and command of language, a peculiar power for analysing human nature and generally strong mental will and determination.

I can add to this statement that if the upper line appears more or less straight across the hand, such persons develop great control over themselves. If, however, this upper line is found rising upwards towards the Heart Line, one side of the nature becomes hard and in some cases cruel, in the carrying out of a purpose whatever it may be; while at the same time the other side of the nature remains excessively gentle and sensitive.

On a soft or effeminate type of hand, the lower Head Line may be found descending over and into the Mount of Luna, thus accentuating the feminine characteristics. In such cases a man with this 'double Line of Head' may be found on the one hand to employ all the gentleness, tenderness and emotional qualities usually ascribed to women. In all such cases persons with the 'double Line of Head' are inclined to live what are called 'double lives' of one form or another. In my own particular case for more than twenty years one section of the public only knew me under my *nom de guerre* of Cheiro, while another knew me only under my own name.

### The Line of Head in its bearing to the seven types of hand

The Line of Head is generally found more or less in accordance with the type of hand on which it is found, namely practical or level on a practical type, or sloping downwards towards the Mount of Luna on the artistic or imaginative class.

There are seven types of hand ranging from the elementary or lowest, to what is called the 'mixed hand', where the formation of each individual finger appears to belong to one type or another.

These types will be found fully described and illustrations given at the beginning of this book.

In this chapter we have to consider them in relation to the indications of mentality as shown by the Line of Head.

The rule to bear in mind is, that any variations in this line not in accordance with the character of the hand on which it is found, gives greater importance to the meaning of the variations whatever they may be.

For example, on an elementary hand or lowest type, the natural Head Line would be a short, heavy, thick or coarse-looking line. If, however, such a hand had a long well-marked Head Line, the natural inference is that the person has developed a mentality far above what would ordinarily have been expected.

As the square hand gives qualities of the materialistic or practical nature, it is reasonable to expect to find a Line of Head of that order, namely straight on the palm, or what is called 'level-headed'. It therefore follows that if the Head Line on such a hand appears bending or sloping towards the Mount of Luna, some unusual inventive faculties would be indicated.

The spatulate hand is itself the hand of invention and originality. Therefore a sloping or imaginative Head Line would be more or less in keeping with it, and the combination would be natural. If, on the contrary, the Head Line were found straight or level across the palm, such practical mentality would hold the original or inventive qualities of the spatulate hand so much in check that originality or invention would not be allowed scope for the exploitation of ideas.

The natural position of the Line of Head on the philosophic hand would be in close conjunction with the Line of Life at the source, giving caution, prudence and thoughtfulness. If therefore found with a wide space between it and the Life Line the reverse qualities would be accentuated by the contradiction between the line and the nature of the hand.

On the conic or artistic hand the natural form of the Head Line will be more or less sloping. If, on the contrary, the Line of Head on such a type were found level or lying straight across, the man or woman would not be a painter, poet or writer, but would more likely make a business of art in some form or other.

On the psychic hand the natural position of the line is extremely sloping, giving the visionary or dreamy qualities. Therefore if found lying straight on such a hand the man or woman would make practical use of their visionary or psychic qualities.

On the mixed hand, namely one where each finger appears to belong to a different type, the most favourable mental indication would be a straight Head Line. This would give the strongest probability of the subject making something out of the versatility which is the basis of the mixed hand.

It must always be borne in mind that the Line of Head appears to divide the hand into two portions or hemispheres. The upper contains the base of the fingers and the fingers themselves representing the intellectual side of the nature while the lower represents the more material side.

A person with long shapely fingers will belong to a higher mental order than a person with short stubby coarse-looking fingers.

The shape of the hands, thumb and fingers I describe fully earlier in this book.

## Criminal propensities shown by the Line of Head

Thieves, forgers and those who prey like vultures on their fellows and deliberately use their brains to defraud others, have, as might be expected, a long Line of Head, but one more or less curving upwards at the end under the Mount of Mercury.

The Mount of Mercury is generally in such cases marked with cross lines like a grid, and the fourth finger appears unusually long and may be slightly crooked towards the top phalange. The fingers on such a hand are also long and as a general rule all close together.

If the Line of Head very early at its commencement throws a line from it towards or into the Mount of Saturn, a leaning or tendency towards crime will manifest in early youth.

It is on such points that an examination of children's hands would be of inestimable value to parents, for it is undoubtedly true that vigilance, understanding and affection have the strongest possible chance of breaking such evil influences before they get too strong a hold on impressionable youth.

I would advise the student to examine carefully the indications I have called attention to in this chapter.

As previously stated, the Line of Head divides the hand as it were into two hemispheres, mind and matter.

To be normal it should lie evenly across the palm, neither too long nor too low, with a well-defined space between the head and heart.

If found clinging at its commencement to the Line of Life and sloping rapidly downwards into the palm, the extreme sensitiveness indicated turns the person as it were 'into himself', making the subject feel everything too acutely. He shrinks back from contact with others or with the world in general. The morbid sensitiveness becomes too strong, and if not taken in time, such natures usually turn to suicide as their only escape from the 'slings and arrows of outrageous fortune'.

An example of suicidal mania may be seen among the special impressions of hands showing unbalanced mentality (see Plate 6).

Examples of insanity are shown in Plates 7, 8 and 9.

Propensities towards murder could be classed under so many different heads that the circumstances leading up to it must be considered from the most broad-minded and impartial standpoint.

The fact that one man kills another in a fit of uncontrollable passion or blind fury is more or less an accident that may occur to anyone who has not cultivated self-control.

In such cases the Head Line is generally short and coarse-looking, with a brutal-looking thumb even if not exactly a 'clubbedthumb'.

With such subjects the Line of Head may not shoot upward towards the Heart Line or even send any branch towards it. Murder with such subjects is simply a question of a moment of madness in a fit of ungovernable rage.

There is, however, another class of murderer—that of the brooding, melancholy type. In this class the Head Line is generally shown in a kind of jumble of Head and Heart Lines with a sloping line from this formation to, or towards, the Mount of Luna (Plate 7).

In this case the man would brood for years over some real or fancied wrong, generally proceeding in some way from the affections. Examples may be read in the newspapers almost every day of men who murder their wives and sometimes their entire family.

From the standpoint of study, the most interesting class of murderer is the poisoner. Here calculation, patience, caution, intelligence all play their rôle. In consequence the Line of Head would naturally be expected to be long, finely marked and connected with the Life Line to give it extreme caution.

I have seen the hands of many poisoners in my career, but I never met one who had the Head Line detached from that of life with a space between the two. This latter class would act with too much impulsiveness to be attracted to the poisoner's art, requiring long patience, planning and caution.

In the case of a youth of only nineteen years of age, it was disclosed that for two years previously he had carefully planned to get rid of every member of his immediate family in order to inherit money. For this terrible purpose he had denied himself every pleasure in order to save up and have the means of buying the poison he required.

In this boy's case a branch from the Line of Head ran upward into the Mount of Saturn.

*Plate 1* Cheiro

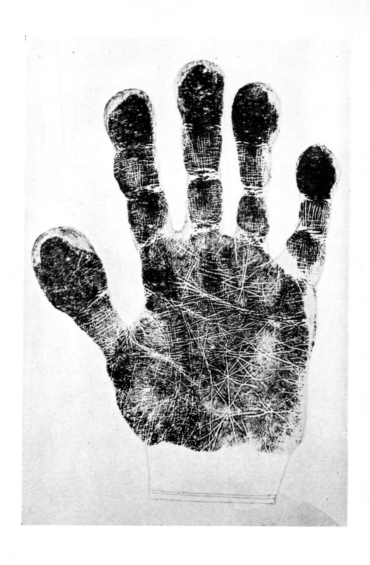

*Plate 2*  Hand of a boy showing malformation of the heart

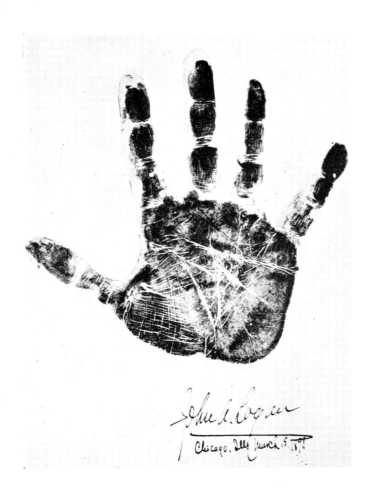

*Plate 3*  The hand of Major John A. Logan. Note the broken line of Head

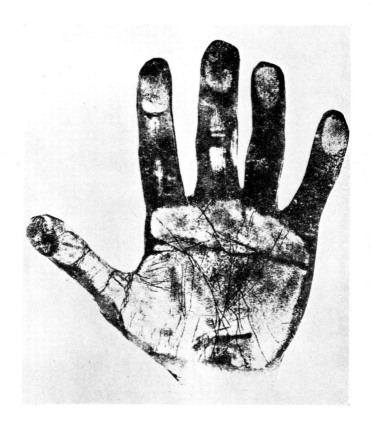

*Plate 4* The hand of Dr. Meyer, the Chicago poisoner

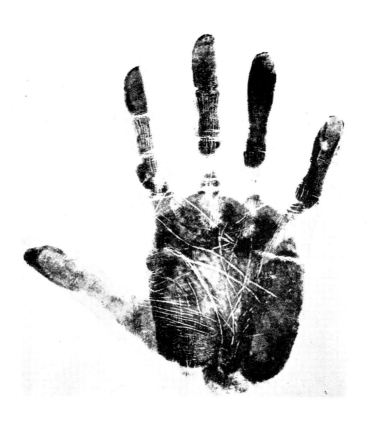

*Plate 5*  Hand showing double line of Head (Cheiro's hand)

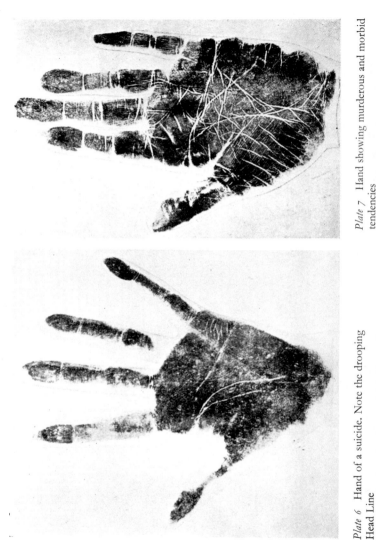

*Plate 6* Hand of a suicide. Note the drooping Head Line

*Plate 7* Hand showing murderous and morbid tendencies

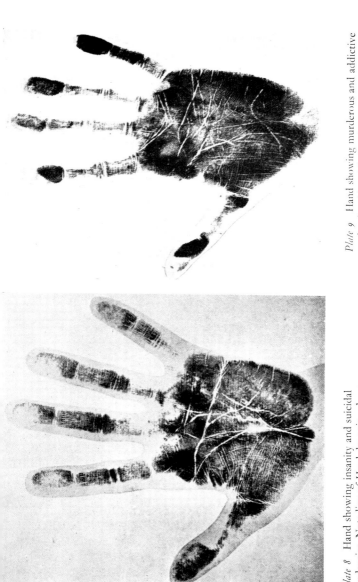

*Plate 8* Hand showing insanity and suicidal tendencies. Note line of Head drooping downwards from centre of palm

*Plate 9* Hand showing murderous and addictive tendencies. Note Via Lasciva

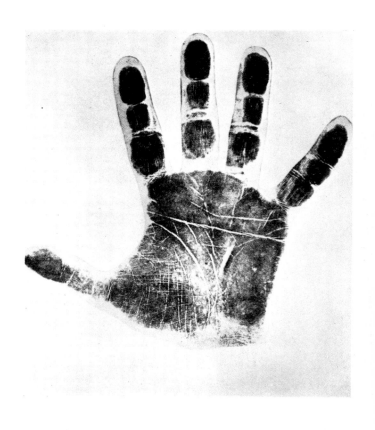

*Plate 10*  Hand showing a strangely eventful career

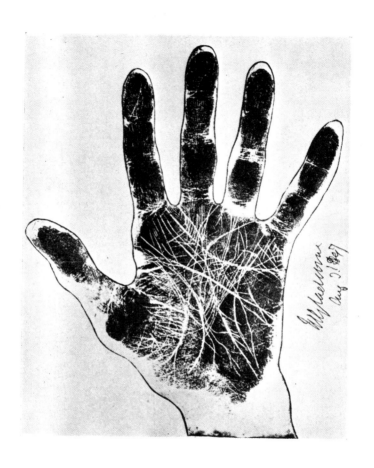

*Plate 11* The hand of Gladstone

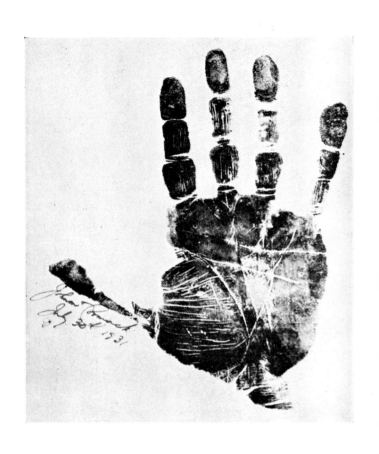

*Plate 12*   The hand of Count John MacCormack

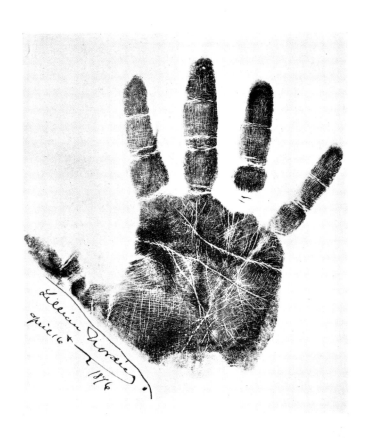

*Plate 13*   The hand of Lillian Nordica

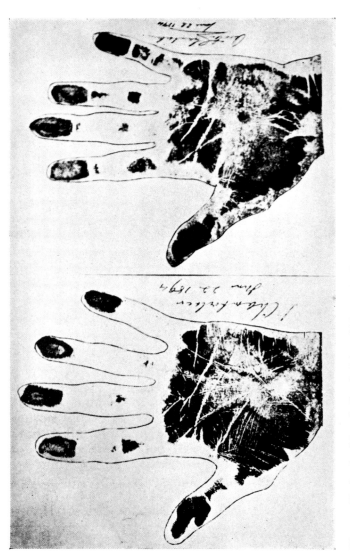

*Plate 14* The hands of Joseph Chamberlain and his son, Sir Austen

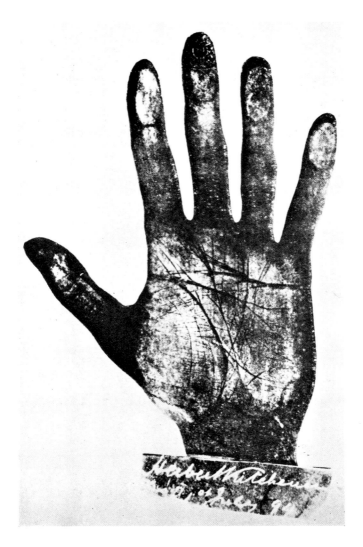

*Plate 15*   The hand of Lord Kitchener

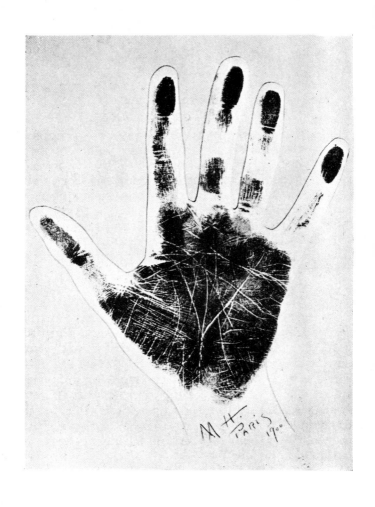

*Plate 16* The hand of Mata Hari

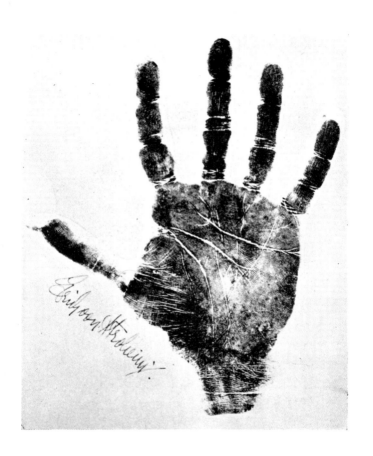

*Plate 17* The hand of Erich von Stroheim

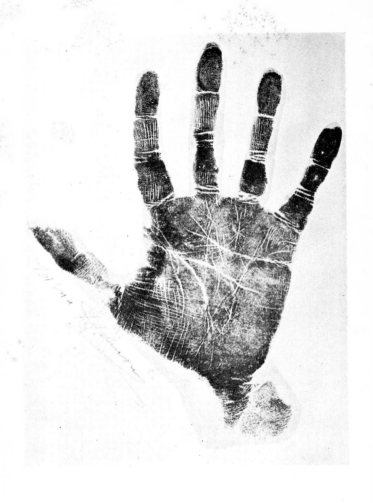

*Plate 18*   The hand of Countess Hamon

The Line of Life is that line which commences under the base of the first finger and circles round the ball of the thumb towards the wrist (map of the hand, Fig. 11 and A, Fig. 24.)

This is a line which seldom receives its just due, for it tells so much of the character and condition of the life as well as the story of the constitution.

By its length and freedom from 'breaks' or interferences of any kind one is able to judge the vitality and the length of life normally to be anticipated.

Again, like every other line, there are three normal points of commencement. First a line that appears to start high up on the hand from the base of the Mount of Jupiter (B, Fig. 24). The second is the line commencing like a straight track between the mounts before beginning to curve (A, Fig. 24), and the third rises and curves upwards from the Mount of Mars before encircling the Mount of Venus (C and D, Fig. 24).

The first (B, Fig. 24), starting high on the hand, denotes a very early development of the characteristics of ambition. Children with this indication are difficult to hold back. Their minds mature early, and the competitive instinct of ambition manifests itself even in school days. If this type of line looks delicate or formed with an island or chains at the commencement, it indicates that the early life will be more or less delicate as the subject is liable to overtax his strength.

All lines rising from the Line of Life towards the Mount of Jupiter denote periods in the life of an urge upwards to increased work and ambition (E, Fig. 24). If an island is seen in the Life Line underneath any of these lines, it denotes that the effort is almost too great for the strength, and consequently the person should be warned to husband his vital forces as much as possible at the danger period.

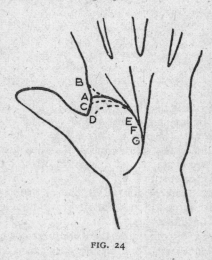

FIG. 24

Lines rising from the Line of Life and bending towards the Mount of Saturn have a totally different meaning. They may not give such ambitious tendencies, but they indicate laborious effort characteristic of the Mount of Saturn (F, Fig. 24).

A line rising from the Line of Life and bending over towards the third finger or the Mount of the Sun is more usually found on the hands of public characters such as orators, actors, statesmen, etc., and is the indication of some supreme effort being made that will crown the work with fame and glory (G, Fig. 24).

The line to the third finger must not be confused with the Line of Health which proceeds downwards from the Mount of Mercury at the base of the fourth finger (see map of the hand). This line, on the contrary, shows opposition to the Life Line or something in the nature undermining the vitality. When the Line of Health or a branch from it comes across and touches the Life Line it is always a dangerous indication of ill health at the time when the Life and Health Lines meet. The Line of Health will be dealt with fully later on.

The second commencement of the Line of Life is the one that appears to lie level between the Mounts of Jupiter and Mars (A, Fig. 24).

This is the most usual of the three types. As a rule it shows a stronger early commencement—unless of course it appears in the form of islands or even a chain—a childhood that is stronger and more robust. This type of Life Line usually takes a wider curve round the Mount of Venus than the others, and if it continues clear and well defined to the end it is a good promise of a robust healthy constitution.

As every line partakes of the nature of the Mount on which it rises, so the Life Line rising from the Mount of Mars indicates a life fretted by the quarrelsome and irritable temperament of the subject (D, Fig. 24).

It is a curious characteristic of this Mars governed Life Line that the subject is continually running into danger as if fascinated by it. Children with such a sign should be carefully guarded against having firearms or explosives or weapons of any kind as they will cause injury to themselves or other people.

Short lines cutting the Line of Life either in an upward or downward direction must not be confused with what are called travel lines.

## Travel lines from the Line of Life

Lines indicating travel or voyages are found in two positions on the hand—one the fine lines dropping or coming out of the Line of Life in a downward direction (A, Fig. 25), and those fine lines in a horizontal position on the lower part of the Mount of Luna (B, Fig. 25).

In some hands travel lines are not shown at all although the subject is much travelled. In most cases this is due to the person not being in any way influenced by the travel he undertakes.

To sailors, travel or voyages become so monotonous and so much a matter of course that it is often impossible to find any trace of them. When, however, the Line of Life itself divides

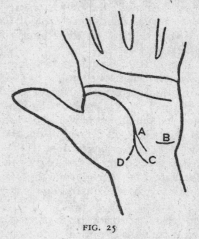

FIG. 25

towards the end and the outer or Travel Line is seen more distinctly marked than the main Line of Life, then the person will leave his native country or direction of place of birth and settle in some opposite part of the world (C, Fig. 25). If the Line of Life remains the stronger and sweeps back to a position underneath where it started, then the person may live abroad at different times for long periods and yet in the end return to the homeland or in the direction of the place of birth (D, Fig. 25).

When these travel lines from the Line of Life end in an island, the voyage or travel will end in disappointment or unsuitable conditions (A, Fig. 26). If the Line of Travel ends in a distinct cross on the Mount of Luna or even pointing in the direction of a cross, it indicates disaster during the voyage and is generally considered the mark of drowning or fatality at sea (B, Fig. 26).

A Travel Line with a square at the end of it or with a distinct triangle is a sign of preservation in accidents by travel. It may be found on the hands of people who travel a great deal if the travel, voyage or change of place affects them mentally.

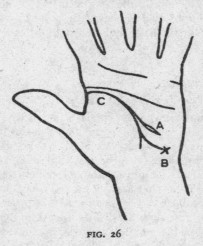

FIG. 26

Naturally water represents only one of the hazards of travel, as accidents can happen when travelling by train, aeroplane or road.

Other signs of accident and violent death are when the Head Line and Fate Line appear broken either when crossing one another or about the centre of the hand. This danger point, however, is as a rule accentuated or confirmed by a line passing from the Mount of Mars near the thumb and itself crossing through the break shown on the Head or Fate Line (C, Fig. 18). This threatens some fatality outside of the person's power to avert, and is one of those remarkable signs indicating violent death by one cause or another.

Another mark of accident is when short deep lines apparently descend from or under the Mount of Saturn and appear to cut through the Line of Life.

A square or a triangle at any of these points of danger is in itself a preservation against the evil effects of such accidents. (More fully explained in the chapter dealing with minor marks and signs.)

A dent or hole or spot in the Life Line is the indication that some shock has injured the vitality at that moment of life. These indentations may, however, be caused by the effect of some sudden illness that may be brought on as a result of an accident.

### The nature of the Line

When the Line of Life appears to be made up of links like a chain it is a sure sign of low vitality and delicacy, particularly if found on a soft hand (A, Fig. 27). When such a line is seen it is very necessary to notice if what is called the double Life Line appears running by its side inside the Line of Life (B, Fig. 27). This double Life Line appears to protect the outer Life Line by the added vitality that it indicates, and I have seen the most delicate people live to a very great age if the inner Life Line is well marked on the right hand. This inner Life Line should be very seriously considered before predicting illness or death.

In some cases it will be noticed that this inner line proceeds for a certain distance fairly close to the outer Life Line, and then retreats from it or leaves the outer line at a certain period. This in itself is an indication that the vitality has in some way or another been undermined, and that the person is no longer able to throw off any illnesses that may be indicated.

This inner Life Line may also show the reverse of all this, for in advancing down the hand it may run closer to the Life Line instead of bending away from it. It can also be found cutting through the Line of Life and passing outwards to the lower part of the Mount of Luna, or sending a branch line in that direction (C, Fig. 27). On a soft hand or one indicating a weak will, this is a very dangerous sign as it indicates a craving for violent excitement obtainable through over-indulgence in alcohol and sometimes in drugs.

In order to be sure that this mark is really an inner Life Line, and not merely a branch from the outer Life Line itself, I advise the student to press this line between both thumbs in the examination, and then it will quickly be seen whether this line proceeds from the outer Life Line or has an independent source.

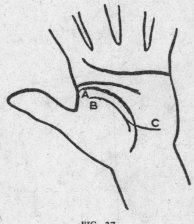

FIG. 27

I recommend this method for examining all other lines, as sometimes the pressure will show either an island or a break that would not be observed in the ordinary way.

When the Life Line is found broken in the left hand and either joined or overlapping in the right, it threatens some dangerous illness at that date. If broken in both hands and there is a gap between the ends of the line, or, worse still, one branch, the upper, curls back on the Mount of Venus, there is hardly any chance that a person will recover from the illness at that period (A, Fig. 28).

When a Line of Life is found with chain formation at its commencement under the first finger, delicate health in the early years is clearly foreshadowed, but if the line becomes clear of this link or chain formation, as it proceeds, it shows that complete recovery from these earlier illnesses may be promised (B, Fig. 28).

When the Line of Life appears closely interwoven with that of the Line of Head it will be found that the subject is extremely sensitive about all things regarding self—the feelings easily hurt because they are so self-centred. If this sign is much accentuated the subject should be encouraged to fight against

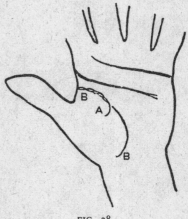

FIG. 28

the foregoing defects and to endeavour to develop more self-confidence and wider interests (A, Fig. 29).

When there is a distinct medium space found between the Line of Life and Line of Head, there appears to be more freedom for the carrying out of plans and ambitions. There is, however, less caution in the character, and more inclination to act on impulse (B, Fig. 29).

If, however, the space is found to be abnormally wide it is an indication of too much self-confidence, and inclines the subject to be foolhardy, impetuous, and inclined to run unusual risks. The life is not guided by reason or caution (C, Fig. 29).

We will now come to the most unusual sign of all, which is that of the Life and Head Lines together with the Line of Heart being all connected together (A, Fig. 30). In such a case it indicates the nature of an extremist. Such people are inclined

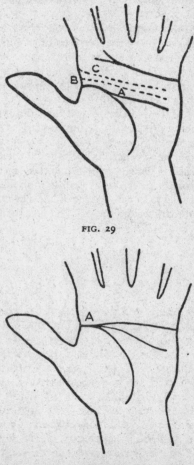

FIG. 29

FIG. 30

to be unfortunate where their affections are concerned. They usually love the wrong person, or those who have what may be called 'tangled lives'. They espouse the cause of the 'under-dog', and stick with the utmost tenacity to what they believe to be their duty to those who have established a claim on their affections.

As a general rule such people love but once in all their life, and that once contains all the elements of tragedy.

The above remarks are all the more emphasised if the Line of Fate should be found rising from the Mount of Venus (A, Fig. 31), or tied down as it were by the Fate and Life Lines being joined together (B, Fig. 31).

If the lines of Life, Head and Heart are found joined on the left hand as shown (A, Fig. 30), but normal in the right, the subject has started with the tendencies described but changed his disposition as he advanced in life. Should the reverse be the case the subject has developed the qualities described.

Another variation of the three lines being joined together is shown in C, Fig. 31. In this the Head and Heart Lines appear as one straight mark across the palm, and at the same time are

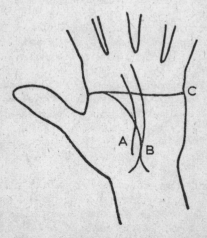

FIG. 31

both joined to the commencement of the Line of Life. This combination, although unusual, may be found on an average in about 1 in 1,000 cases. It has all the qualities of the first described example, but with still more intensity of feelings and disposition. It is as if the person concentrated both head and heart on the one thing that concerned him. If it is love, then all the desires of the life, heart and brain are as one. If it is purpose, then the heart nature is subservient to the mentality.

Such persons are generally unfortunate in the ordinary affairs of life. They do not fit in with the conditions of things around them. They feel lonely because they meet so few like themselves. They are as a rule much misunderstood by everyone they come across. They are inflexible and unchangeable in their views and opinions—they feel 'the world is against them', but it is they who are against the world.

Such persons have unusual brain power, determination, will and concentration, yet all these qualities may amount to nothing unless the lines of Fate and Sun be found on their hands. If such lines appear even late in life such as close to the base of the fingers, success is likely to be achieved before the end. Even then it will be of the nature of something unusual or unexpected.

In all my experience I have, however, never found hands with the Lines of Life, Head and Heart combined, to have morbid or suicidal tendencies. I have known men or women with this mark destined to go through more disappointment and sorrows than thousands of others, but I have never known one of them attempt to shorten his own life—provided no drooping line was found falling downward out of this combination to or towards the Mount of Luna.

As such a sign can, however, be found, I have given an impression of a hand showing this tendency to suicide (Plate 8).

In this case the man, after repeated failure of all his plans, developed an intensely morbid tendency and made several attempts on his own life. In such attempts he was equally unlucky, and spent the remainder of his days under close observation in a mental hospital.

*Chapter 17*   The Line of Heart

The Line of Heart (see map of the hand and Fig. 32) is the line running under the mounts at the base of the fingers.

This line, being on the upper, or intellectual, part of the hand, relates more to what I might call the mental outlook on the affections rather than the physical or sensual.

The Line of Heart may rise from the following distinct positions.

Lying straight across the palm, the Line of Heart denotes an honest, sincere, affectionate disposition, but not one likely to be swayed by any great emotions one way or another.

Rising from the Mount of Mars inside the Life Line (A, Fig. 32) is in itself an unfortunate sign as the character of the person will be irritable, quarrelsome and exacting in all matters of the affections.

Sloping downwards and touching or joining the Life and Head Lines (B, Fig. 32), it is unfortunate from the standpoint that the subject perhaps from lack of perception appears to trust or love the wrong people. He will be inclined to suffer repeated disappointments in those he cares for.

Rising from the centre of the Mount of Jupiter (C, Fig. 32), it denotes a nature exalted in its ideas of affection. Men or women with this sign are firm and reliable in their love nature, ambitious that those they care for may be successful in life. They seldom, if ever, marry beneath their station or rank in life, and as a rule marry above it.

Perhaps because of their pride or high ideals, they will be inclined to have fewer love affairs than those under other indications. This same line coming from the top or outside of the Mount of Jupiter produces an excess of the above qualities. A man or woman with such a line would be a blind enthusiast

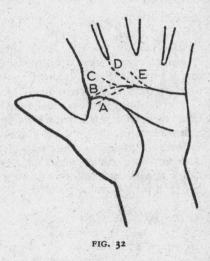

FIG. 32

about any person he or she loved or even cared for. In their pride they can see no faults or failings in the being of their choice. In love they are carried away by their enthusiasm, and often have bitter disappointments when the idol they have worshipped turns out to have 'feet of clay'.

The Line of Heart from between the first and second fingers (D, Fig. 32) is perhaps one of the best signs to have, as it denotes a strong deep nature in matters of the affections. Such persons appear to rest between the ideality given by the Jupiter Line and the solid seriousness given by the Mount of Saturn. They may not be so demonstrative as persons who have the line from Jupiter, but they are deeply in earnest in their protestations and promises.

When the Line of Heart rises on the Mount of Saturn (E, Fig. 32), the subject is more self-contained in his affections. In fact *self* in every sense plays the principal part in such a man or woman's love affairs. They have less ideality about such things than those who have the line from Jupiter. If the hand is soft and flabby they are more inclined to be sensual than affectionate.

All these qualities are in excess when the Line of Heart rises high on the Mount of Saturn.

When the Heart Line is in itself in excess, namely, lying right across the hand from one side to the other, the desire for affection becomes a torment. Such persons love so intensely they cannot bear the person they love to be out of their sight, and therefore continual unhappiness is usually the result.

When the Line of Heart appears with a lot of fine lines dropping down from it as in A, Fig. 33, it denotes an inconsistent nature inclined to fritter away the affections by a series of flirtations or *amourettes*. Such persons must always be 'in love' to live at all, but with them affection is but a name.

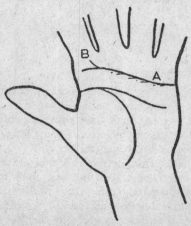

FIG 33

A broad Heart Line either from or under the Mount of Saturn formed by a series of 'islands' denotes there is little or no love for the person's opposite sex. On a soft hand, especially if the Mount of Venus is full and prominent, unnatural desires may be feared.

When the Line of Heart is very low down, on the palm with lines connecting it to that of Head, the affairs of the heart will always mix themselves up with those of the head, and a general muddle of things will be the result.

When the Line of Heart commences on the Mount of Jupiter with a clear, distinct fork (B, Fig. 33), it is an excellent sign of success in love; also of a happy disposition in all questions of the affections. Such persons are inclined to 'make the best of everything', even of their own disappointments.

The Line of Heart found with a wide fork at the commencement (A, Fig. 34), one branch on Jupiter, the other between the first and second fingers, is also an excellent sign of an affectionate disposition that is well balanced. When the fork is found extremely large with one branch of the Mount of Jupiter, the other on Saturn (B, Fig. 34), the subject will have

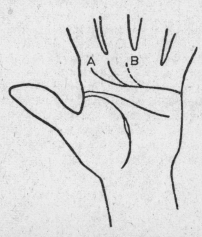

FIG. 34

a contradictory nature in matters of the affections, swayed as it were between the qualities of Jupiter and Saturn.

Such persons will be difficult to live with and to understand. They will be both sensual and idealistic, selfish and generous, demonstrative or the reverse, according to the mood of the moment.

If the Line of Heart is seen devoid of all branches, and just a thin-looking line, the man or woman will have little affection or the desire for it.

When appearing as if it was fading out or becoming slighter at the end under the fourth finger, it denotes that advancing age will bring sterility in the affections, cold-heartedness and indifference.

If on looking at a hand it is observed that the Heart Line appears to stand out as the most important or deeply marked line on the palm, it will be found that the love nature is all that matters to such persons; but with a good Head Line and the rest of the hand well marked this love nature is likely to find its outlet in self-sacrifice for others, especially those in suffering. Such persons make wonderful missionaries, helpers, nurses, prison visitors or workers among the poor.

My last word of advice to those interested in this study is that they should carefully observe the other main lines of the hand before passing judgment on one particular mark or indication. To learn what each line means separately is absolutely necessary to have a good foundation. It is what technique is to music. The musician studies in detail the components that go to make the whole, but eventually reads at a glance all the tones, semi-tones, harmonies and discords on the written sheet. Just so will the student after some practice group and read together the chords or discords of life as shown by the lines on the human hands.

The Line of Health (see map of the hand, also Figs. 35 and 36) is that line which rises on the Mount of Mercury under the fourth finger, or passes under the base of this mount and proceeds down the hand towards the Line of Life.

I have proved by long experience of the study of the hand that this line grows downwards, and that it may increase or fade out in accordance with the state of health of the subject.

The logical reason for this line to grow downwards is that it is, as it were, the enemy of the Life Line, and as it approaches or sends branches on or towards the Line of Life, so one can read whether it is undermining the vitality or not.

As it grows down the palm towards the Line of Life, so does it foreshadow the growth or germ of disease which reaches its crucial point when it comes into contact with the Line of Life. It is an excellent sign of vitality when there is no Line of Health found on a hand. Its absence indicates that there is nothing in the constitution undermining the Line of Life.

The Line of Health may be found rising from various points.

As the Mount of Mercury is proved to have a definite connection with the mind, when the Line of Health is found rising from this position it indicates that the nervous system is more easily affected by the mind than when the line starts on any other position on the palm.

I am speaking intentionally of the *mind* in the case of this line, and not the brain or mentality as represented by the Line of Head.

In this study there appears to be a distinction between the two, as the line from Mercury representing the mind may in many cases be found deeply marked on a hand where the Head Line is only slightly marked or does not show mental power of any consequence.

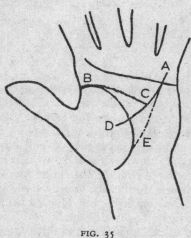

FIG. 35

The Line of Health rising on the Mount of Mercury (A, Fig. 35), apart from any other consideration denotes an active sensitive mind.

Now bring the Head Line into the picture, and at once a wealth of information as to the inner meaning of the Line of Health becomes apparent.

For example, should the Line of Health, as in A, Fig. 35, be found on a hand with a weak uncertain-looking Line of Head (B, Fig. 35), then the mind as indicated by the Line of Health on Mercury is fretful and of a worrying nature, that as it were eats up the vitality and produces ill-health. In this case there may not be any real disease that a doctor could put his finger on, and yet such a person may feel as wretched and as ill as if some real malady was devouring the constitution.

Should this Line of Health (A, Fig. 35) send a branch from it to the Line of Life (C, Fig. 35), and if this branch line cuts into or touches the Line of Life at any part, a serious breakdown may be expected in the subject's constitution, or such a 'run-down' condition that even death may be the result at the date on the Line of Life where the two lines meet (D, Fig. 35).

If the Line of Health itself proceeds down the palm, the life may be a long one, but the fretful, highly sensitive conditions will remain to the end (E, Fig. 35).

Let us now consider the opposite of this. If even with a weak-looking Line of Head, the Health Line does not approach the Line of Life, or even bends away from it, the nature though fretful and troubled will not damage the life and end it at a premature age (A, Fig. 36).

An 'island' at the commencement of the Line of Health on the Mount of Mercury increases the bad indication given by this line, especially during the early years (B, Fig. 36).

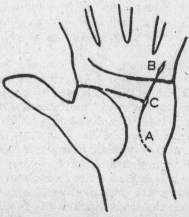

FIG. 36

An 'island' lower down, touching or passing through the end of a weak-looking Head Line, increases the weak indications of the Head Line, and at the same time threatens some form of brain illness (C, Fig. 36).

When on the contrary a Line of Health is found rising on the Mount of Mercury with a long, straight Line of Head on the same hand, the mind, although of the most active, highly sensitive type, becomes under the control of the mental will-power, and so a Line of Health on such a hand is prevented from wearing out the vital forces by useless fretful imaginings (A, Fig. 37). This condition will be accentuated if the Line of Head rises on or has a branch from the Mount of Jupiter (B, Fig. 37).

Even in this case, however, the mind being of the excessively sensitive order with the Line of Health coming from Mercury, the subject will always have a *self-worrying tendency about the mental work the brain is engaged upon.* He will be inclined to be super-critical, never satisfied with his best efforts, and if the Line of Health continues down the hand from Mercury, whether it touches the Line of Life or not it will induce periodic nervous exhaustion and a high-strung condition all through his life.

Such subjects always work at high pressure—are over-conscientious in all they are called on to do, and are inclined to wear themselves out by attempting too much for their physical strength.

Should any 'island' appear on the Line of Life (C, Fig. 37) of a person who has the Health Line from Mercury as shown by A, Fig. 37, it denotes the loss of vital force at the date when the 'island' appears, but not of such a critical nature as if a branch from the Line of Health should cross from it towards the Line of Life at that period.

If on such a person's hand the Line of Life seems to split at its termination into a formation like 'hair-lines' (D, Fig. 37), the nerve force will be broken up or dissipated towards the end of the life.

The fretful or irritable condition would be ten times more increased if lines from the Mount of Mars should be seen running up into the Line of Head at its commencement (E, Fig. 37).

When the Line of Health rises from the Line of Heart out of an 'island' it foretells some weakness of the heart, but generally of a nervous, excitable nature.

When this line is only seen on the upper part of the hand and appears to fade out from under the Head Line or centre of the palm, the person will recover about the middle of his

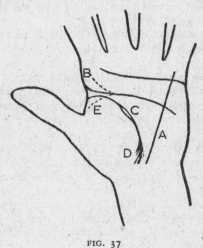

FIG. 37

life from whatever tendencies the Line of Health denoted in the early years.

When this line is only found at the Head Line and from then on is strongly marked, nervous illness will be brought on by the particular mental work the person is engaged in.

When the Line of Health is found split in little pieces with each piece approaching nearer the Line of Life, it denotes periods of overstrain of the nervous system, and if the nails on such a hand appear flat or shell shape (see chapter on nails, Part I), some form of paralysis is to be feared.

When the Line of Health is seen with a series of islands in it between the Heart and Head Lines, and at the same time the person has round-shaped nails, trouble with the throat and bronchial tubes may be expected. With long filbert-shaped nails, the 'islands' foreshadow delicacy of the lungs, such as pleurisy and danger of tuberculosis.

It will thus be seen that although the student can open up a mine of information from the indications of health and disease given by the study of this mysterious line, he can gain added information not only from the Line of Life, but also from the nails on the fingers.

As explained before, judgment should not be passed on any single mark by itself without taking into consideration other lines or signs that may bear on the subject in question.

An examination of the Line of Health is especially useful for parents, if they would know in advance the physical constitution of the children they have brought into the world.

The Line of Fate (see map of the hand—and Figs. 38, 39 and 40), or, as it is also called, the Line of Destiny, is the centre line running from the direction of the wrist to or towards the base of the second finger.

In the examination of this line, the type of hand on which it is found must be considered.

It is not so strongly marked on the elementary, square or spatulate as it is on the philosophic, conic or psychic. For this reason, if it is found at all on the first-named hands, or if even slightly marked on them, it will have just as much importance as a strong Line of Fate on the later mentioned types.

Strange to say, the possessors of the philosophic, conic or psychic hands, which as a rule bear the Fate Line more distinctly marked than the others, are in themselves more fatalistic than those who have the elementary, square or spatulate. Being more spiritual, more thoughtful, more visionary, they are naturally believers in destiny.

Properly speaking, the Line of Fate is more closely related to one's worldly affairs, success or failure, people who influence one's career, the difficulties or barriers to be met with in one's aims and so forth.

There are many points from which the Line of Fate may commence.

From the wrist, and going straight up to the base of the Mount of Saturn (A, Fig. 38), it promises strong individuality of the self-centred class. Provided the other indications are good, it denotes a successful destiny, and the accomplishment of one's purpose, whatever that may be. On account of the space between this line and that of Life it shows that the

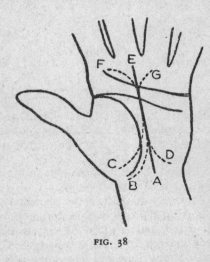

FIG. 38

subject has not been tied down or fettered by unfortunate conditions, but has been free to choose his or her career.

When lying very close to the Life Line, or as it were tied down by it (B, Fig. 38), home surroundings and ties of relationship have stood in the way, and the subject has been much sacrificed in the early life to the wishes of others. This condition is very often seen on the hand of a daughter who has given up her own ambitions for the sake of remaining with or helping a parent.

Rising inside the Line of Life on Venus (C, Fig. 38), the cramping of the early years has been still more marked, and unless the Fate Line looks exceptionally strong in the later years as it ascends beyond the Line of Head, the subject will always be held back with relations or by ties of affection in one form or another.

It is a curious thing, but well worth noting, that if any of these Fate Lines tied down by the Line of Life or rising from Venus are found on a hand with a Heart Line sloping downwards from its commencement (B, Fig. 32), the subject will be most unfortunate in all matters concerned with the affections.

Men or women with such Fate Lines as a general rule get tangled up in their love affairs with other persons who are married, or at least not free to marry.

The Line of Fate may also rise from any part of the Mount of Luna (D, Fig. 38). In such a case the person has had no family ties in early years to hold him back. He has been free from home influences. As a rule such people have restless, wandering lines, and generally travel a great deal all through their careers. Their fate will be considerably influenced by the caprice or whims of others. On a hand with the rest of the lines favourable, this class of Fate Line can be very fortunate, especially in the case of public favourites.

At the other end of the Line of Fate the terminations are equally important.

The Line running straight into the Mount of Saturn (E, Fig. 38) is not nearly so powerful or lucky in its meaning as if the same line had bent over towards Jupiter (F. Fig. 38). In the latter case the man or woman would attain to some position of authority over others, or his or her destiny would be so successful that he would reach the highest possible positions in whatever his profession or career might be.

The Line of Fate turning towards or sending a branch from it to the Mount of Sun (G, Fig. 38), is a promise of unusual success, glory or fame, especially in public life in one form or another.

A remarkable example of this may be seen in the hand of the Right Hon. W. E. Gladstone. In his case the Line of Fate actually divides, one branch going to Jupiter and the other to the Mount of the Sun (Plate II).

On his hand will be noticed the wide space between the commencement of the Line of Fate and that of Life, denoting how unfettered and free he was at the beginning of his destiny to choose his career. Although by nature extremely sensitive—see Head and Life Lines closely connected—he adopted a public career as a statesman. He held the highest positions in the Government of England, and was no less than four times Prime Minister.

When I took this impression of his remarkable hand (the only one ever taken), I visited Mr. Gladstone at his request at his home, Hawarden Castle, in the county of Cheshire. He was keenly interested in the various impressions of famous persons' hands I had taken with me. We passed upwards of two hours together. It was one of the last interviews he ever gave as he passed to his long rest the following year.

Mr. Gladstone's hand contains a wonderful lesson for the student of this work. It is not only a remarkable example of a Head Line across the entire palm, of a Fate Line going to the Mounts of Jupiter and the Sun, but also of the 'double Line of Life' at the back of the outer Life Line.

Mr. Gladstone lived to the great age of eighty-six. He had such remarkable strength and vitality to the end that he actually chopped down a large oak tree in his park a few months before he passed away.

If at any point in the Line of Fate it throws a branch to or towards the Mount of Jupiter, it denotes that at that period of the person's fate, he or she will make some extra effort towards ambition (A, Fig. 39). If the offshoot should be towards the Mount of the Sun, increase of riches, distinct success, fame or publicity may be expected (B, Fig. 39).

If the Line of Fate should go right up into the finger of Saturn, it is not favourable, for this signifies that everything will go too far. If a man who had this mark were a leader of men, the day would come when they would get beyond his control and turn against him.

If the Line of Fate stops abruptly at the Line of Heart it foretells that the destiny will be ruined by the affections. If stopped by the Line of Head, some mental action will injure the destiny, or it will be thwarted by the person's own stupidity.

When the Line of Fate appears with an island or islands at its commencement, it denotes trouble or misfortune early in the destiny (C, Fig. 39).

Short lines like bars that are seen crossing the Fate (D, Fig. 39) are usually the opposition of some person to one's destiny at that particular period. (How to read times and dates explained in Chapter 25.)

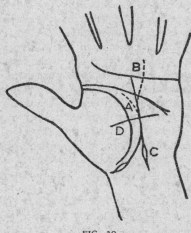

FIG. 39

These opposition lines from the Mount of Mars under the Line of Life or the Mount of Venus usually signify men, when found on a man's hand, or women, when found on a women's hand, who will endeavour to do some injury to the subject at the particular date on which these lines appear to cross the Line of Fate.

If the Line of Fate does not rise until about the middle of the palm, from what is termed the Plain of Mars, it denotes a hard difficult life in the early part of the existence. If from there on the line looks clear and straight, the difficulties will be overcome by the person's own strength of individuality and determination.

When the Line of Fate rises from the Line of Head, and from that is well marked, success will come from about middle life from the individual's own application or mental effort.

When rising from the Line of Heart, success will come very late in life, and generally in some way by or through the affections.

If the Line of Fate rises with one branch on Venus, the other on the Mount of Luna, the subject's destiny will be swayed between Romance and Imagination on the one side and Passion and Sensuality on the other (A, Fig. 40).

When there is a complete break in the Line of Fate, it is a sure sign of loss and misfortune, but if one line begins before the other leaves off, it promises a complete change of career at that date. If from then the second line appears strong and clear, the change will be for the person's advantage, and will probably be in accordance with his or her own desires (B, Fig. 40).

A distinct cross (C, Fig. 40) at the end of the Fate Line on

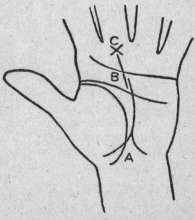

FIG. 40

Saturn is one of the most unfortunate signs to be found. Such a person's career will be dogged by ill-luck of every kind and will end badly.

If with such a mark the Line of Head should show murderous tendencies as explained in the chapter dealing with Head Lines, then the cross on Saturn would foreshadow death by violence, such as by the hand of the executioner.

A double Fate Line is often an excellent sign, especially if one branch goes to Jupiter and the other to the Mount of the Sun (A, Fig. 41). As a rule it shows that the person will run two different careers side by side, but on a woman's hand it usually denotes what is called a 'double life', especially if one of these Fate Lines comes from the Mount of Venus. On a man's hand this sign is very rarely found, but if found it gives the same meaning.

Long or short fine lines rising by the side of the Fate Line, joining it or running by the side of it, show the influence of some person or persons of the opposite sex on one's destiny (B, Fig. 41). If the Fate Line appears to improve after the influence line comes into it, the person represented by the influence line will be favourable. If on the contrary the Fate

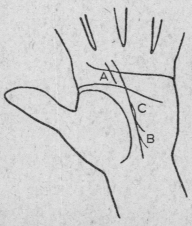

FIG. 41

Line has an island in it, or looks slighter when the influence line joins it, the person will bring one harm or loss (C, Fig. 41).

If the influence line has itself an 'island' in it, the person drawn into one's fate will have had misfortune or disgrace in his or her own career.

When the Line of Fate divides into branches or a series of lines about the centre of the hand, it indicates that the career will branch out into many different phases. Some of these parallel activities will be more successful than others, as will be seen if each branch is studied as a separate line.

Persons whose hands show no Line of Fate whatever can still be successful provided the Head Line is well marked. Their careers will, however, be more or less monotonous and uneventful.

The Line of Sun—also called the Line of Success (see map of the hand and Figs. 42 and 43)—should, like the Line of Fate, be considered with the type of hand on which it is found.

It is more generally seen clearly marked on the philosophic, conic and psychic, and does not mean so much as even a lesser-looking line on the square or spatulate. I must stress this point so as to bring out the meaning of this most important mark, which has been more badly interpreted than any other line on the hand.

In Greek works on Cheiromancy, this line is called 'the Line of Apollo', for the reason that Apollo was identified with the sun god Helios.

In my work I have preferred to call it by the simple name of the Line of Sun or Success. It appears to take after the qualities of the God of Life, in that when well marked on a hand, it becomes like the Sun to the Earth in bringing into fruition the aims and desires of the individual.

It increases the promise of success by a good Line of Fate in the way that it gives distinction, brightness and in some cases fame and glory to the career. As the Sun brings fertility, and consequently riches to the earth, so this Line of the Sun improves the worldly position of the person on whose hand it may be found.

Now, as everything in life must be judged by comparison, this line must be judged by the conditions governing the career of the man or woman under examination.

I mean by this that if this line is seen appearing at a certain age in the hand of, say, a shopkeeper, it does not mean that he will suddenly become an Imperial potentate having the power of life and death over his subjects, but merely that he was assured of a period of success in business that would make him feel a king among his fellows, and so on in connection with every other career or activity that may be imagined.

To the poor artist, up to then starving in some attic, it would show when his pictures would begin to be recognised. To the writer the period when his books would bring him fame. To the actor the age at which he would make his mark. To the clergyman when he would receive clerical recognition. To the businessman when the 'tide had turned'. To even the 'woman of the streets' when her luck would change.

To high or low, king or peasant, to one or all, irrespective of birth, rank or education, whenever the Line of Sun appears there will be *an improvement in conditions* in due accordance with whatever the career may be.

To my mind it is the most wonderful line on the hand, and also the most difficult for the amateur to 'read'.

The Line of Sun is so many-sided in the way it can be applied to the affairs of everyday life that I could write a volume on it alone. In a work of this nature I must limit myself to its principle indications, giving the student a solid foundation from my own practical experience in the hope that out of the many who will read these pages there will be a few who will find a mine of wisdom and the pure gold of knowledge.

The mysterious statement 'many are called but few are chosen' applies to all the devotees of scientific research.

The Line of Sun may rise from the Line of Life (A, Fig. 42); the Mount of Luna (B, Fig. 42); the centre of the palm known as the Plain of Mars (C, Fig. 42); the Line of Fate (D, Fig. 42);

the Line of Head (E, Fig. 42); or from any part of the Line of Heart (F, Fig. 42).

Rising from the Line of Life, if the rest of the hand belongs to the artistic type, the life will be devoted to the worship of the beautiful, and if the Line of Head is sloping and well marked it promises success in artistic pursuits.

Rising from the Mount of Luna the success and distinction will be largely dependent upon the approbation of others,

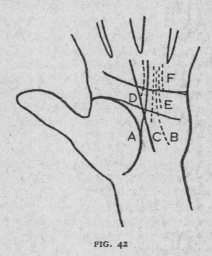

FIG. 42

especially when the Line of Fate also rises from this direction. This indication is most often found in the hands of public favourites who excite the adoration of the multitude.

Rising from the centre of the hand on the Plain of Mars (C, Fig. 42), the Line of Sun promises sunshine after tears, success after battling with adversity.

When coming out of the Line of Fate itself (D, Fig. 42), no matter from what part it makes its departure, it accentuates the success promised by the Line of Fate. From that time on everything concerning the career will improve.

When the Line of Sun is seen rising from the Line of Head

(E, Fig. 42), no caprice of others is involved in connection with the success promised. The talents and brain power of the person alone will be the deciding factor, but in this position fame or success will not be gained until after the middle of life is reached.

Rising from the Line of Heart (F, Fig. 42), it may only denote great love and talent for artistic things, but in its other meaning it promises that there will be greater sunshine, happiness or money in the person's life from that date on. Should, however, the Line of Fate turn towards the Mount of Jupiter at the same time, then the late Sun Line may be translated as meaning some unusual success of the nature of position in the world, or authority over others from then to the end of life.

Many lines on the Mount of Sun show a decidedly artistic nature and a certain amount of success late in life, but these many lines also tell that multiplicity of ideas or pursuits interfere with great success. One or two lines in this position are preferable to having a good many.

A star on the Mount of Sun (A, Fig. 43) at any place is one of the best promises that can be found—if towards the termination of the line on the Mount of the Sun great fame or glory is assured.

It must be borne in mind that, as its name implies, publicity or the 'limelight' of life is found more in the careers of those who have the line of Sun accentuated, than in cases where it is only lightly shown.

In hands badly marked such as those with criminal or unfortunate tendencies, the Line of Sun may give too much publicity or notoriety of an unenviable kind.

A square on the Line of Sun (B, Fig. 43) is a sign of preservation from the attacks of those who would endeavour to ruin one's name or reputation.

An island on the Line of Sun (C, Fig. 43) indicates loss of position and reputation so long as the island lasts. If the line appears as strong after the island as it was up to that time, it promises that the person will completely recover from whatever the scandal or trouble may have been.

Lines crossing the hand from the Mount of Mars and

cutting or breaking the Line of Sun denote persons of one's own sex endeavouring to injure one's position or reputation (D, Fig. 43).

Lines from the Mount of Venus or Mars, crossing over and cutting the Line of Sun, tell in a man's hand of men who will injure him, especially if any form of island be shown at the same time.

On a woman's hand these lines from Venus or Mars mean

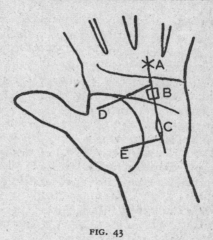

FIG. 43

her own sex will injure her reputation or position. If an island be marked at the same time some decided scandal is indicated at the date in the life when the 'island' appears (E, Fig. 43).

When there is a strongly marked Line of Fate, but no sign of any Line of Sun whatever, the Fate Line may promise power and success in whatever the career may be, but there will be little brightness or happiness in the life. The man or woman will be extremely self-centred. They will shun publicity of all kinds, and will show little or no desire to enter social life.

When the Sun Line appears stronger on a hand than the Line of Fate, the person is overshadowed by the fame or glory of his forbears. This is often seen on the hands of sons who have famous fathers. An unusually good example of this was seen in the right hand of Prince Louis Napoleon. When a General in the Russian army he was deliberately kept in the background by the 'powers that be' for fear of complications with France on account of the famous name he bore.

When I pointed out the significance of the Line of Sun in his hand, he said: 'You are quite right, Cheiro  The weight of carrying an illustrious name is the greatest burden a man can have.'

The Line of Sun should be equally balanced with the Line of Fate; if it appears unusually strongly marked, the career will be full of promise of brilliancy and fame, but without as it were any solid foundation.

The intricate and fascinating story of marriage is written on the hand in many different ways, and in accordance with the temperament of the subject under examination.

On the question of marriage as revealed by the lines of the hand, the student must realise that he is not a judge, but the counsellor and friend of the subject whose love-life is stripped of secrecy in his palms. He must take the broadest possible view of the question if he is to deserve the privilege of probing into the inner sanctuaries of the mind and heart. It is human to love and to desire love.

No two life-stories are alike. The student must humbly refrain from 'sitting in judgment', and read without shirking all he sees without comment save warning, sympathy, and if he be competent to give it—advice.

It is useless for the student to attempt to study what the hands tell of love and marriage till he has cleared his mind of all prejudice, and acquired the breadth of vision which is necessary to understanding. People think and act and live according to their lights, their environment and their early training, but all humanity is struggling upwards towards a finer social system, a higher ideal of love. Each individual seeks and hopes for perfection as he or she sees it.

Some are born mature, with an innate wisdom which is beautifully applied to the great art of living, while others are little more than children at the end of their lives. There is no life experience which proves this theory more strongly than the individual attitude to marriage, the personal reaction to love. For this reason the student must recognise that where one subject will believe that marriage is no sacrament unless solemnised in a church, another will be satisfied to be married by a registrar, a third will prefer a Gretna Green marriage over an anvil to a ceremony at an altar, while a fourth will hold that love itself is sanctification enough, and find in an 'irregular union' a spiritual inspiration.

Again, there are cases in which in spite of the deep desire of the subject, legal marriage is prevented by circumstances, yet the ties of affection remain equally strong. And there are others where no beauty of ceremony nor vows blessed by Church have been successful in capturing and imprisoning love. It is well to bear in mind that morality is not a fixed thing, but is determined by location. What is moral in one country is immoral in another, and much so-called marriage has nothing to do with love.

All reasoning minds admit that there must be marriage laws to protect children and stabilise the social system which exists for the greatest good of the greatest number. But the fact that many a human heart chafes in its fetters, or cannot love within the rigid confines of the law, should rouse sympathy not censure, and call for guidance rather than judgment from the student whose skill exposes the secret of suffering.

Some of the greatest idealists make the unhappiest unions. The lines of the palm appear to indicate that they were 'fated' to do so, yet at the same time show that had the subject waited he would have met his real affinity and life-long happiness would have been assured.

The most important indications of unions or marriages are given by 'the marriage lines' on the Mount of Mercury, which is again in keeping with how the *mind* reacts to the idea of marriage.

The Line of Marriage should lie straight and clear on the

Mount of Mercury (A, Fig. 44). Only the long or important-looking lines on this mount relate to marriage or long unions—short lines relate to affairs that do not result in marriage.

On the Line of Fate if marriage has occurred at the period of age indicated on the Mount of Mercury, we may find it corroborated, and information given as to the effect the marriage has produced, which I will proceed to explain a little later.

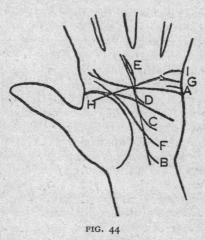

FIG. 44

From the position of the line on the Mount of Mercury, a fair idea of the age of the person at the time the marriage took place or will take place may be obtained. For instance, when a strongly marked line is found lying rather close to the Line of Heart, the union will be early, between fifteen to twenty (A, Fig. 44).

Half-way up the mount, twenty-five to thirty, higher up still forty-five to fifty-five and so on. If an influence line is seen joining the Line of Fate, it will give a more exact date (B, Fig. 44). Here is shown an influence line joining the Line of Fate very early at about eighteen to twenty years of age.

At the centre of the hand on or about where the Fate and

Head Lines cross is considered the middle of the fate; an influence line joining it at this period would be considered to be about thirty-five years of age (C, Fig. 44). On the Mount of Mercury this should be corroborated by a line about the middle of the Mount. How time or dates of events are placed in the hand will be explained later in a special chapter dealing with the matter.

If the Fate Line appears to improve or look stronger when or after the influence line has joined it, the marriage has been favourable and improved the material position.

If, on the contrary, the Line of Fate is broken, irregular or badly marked after the influence line has joined it, and if this influence line tallies with the date given for the Marriage Line on the Mount of Mercury, then the reverse has been the case.

A wealthy union may in this way be judged by the Line of Fate, or if a Line of Sun is seen opposite the joining of the influence line to the fate, which is very often the case.

When the line of influence comes decidedly from the Mount of Luna, the marriage or union will be more from the standpoint of capricious fancy than if the line of influence appears close to the Line of Fate.

When the influence line looks stronger than the subject's own Line of Fate, the person the subject marries will have the stronger individuality of the two.

One of the happiest signs of marriage is when the influence line continues as a fine attendant line by the side of the Line of Fate (D, Fig. 44), provided that the Marriage Line on the Mount of Mercury is straight and well marked.

If, however, the line of influence has an 'island' in it or runs into one (E, Fig. 44), it denotes that the person who influences the fate will get into trouble of a serious kind. If at the same time an island appears in the Line of Sun it will be of the nature of some public scandal.

If the influence line passes through the Line of Fate and proceeds towards the Mount of Jupiter, the person on whose hand it is found will be sacrificed to the ambitions of the partner (F, Fig. 44).

The Marriage Line on the Mount of Mercury (A, Fig. 44)

should be level and without breaks or crosses of any kind. If found like this it promises a happy marriage.

When found divided into two fine lines, it denotes that the two people may continue to live together but they will have divided interests (G, Fig. 44). This is not a bad sign in itself, and only becomes so if a Line of Mars crosses from the Mount into this division (H, Fig. 44).

If the Marriage Line in itself curves or drops downwards it foretells the loss of the partner through death (I, Fig. 44).

If the Line of Marriage curves downwards into a fork (A, Fig. 45), it is an indication of unhappiness in married life. When a line crosses from Mars into such a mark, the probability is that divorce will end the marriage (B, Fig. 45).

If the Line of Marriage is connected with a line from the Mount of Venus (C, Fig. 45), the influence of the subject's own sex will interfere with the marriage.

When the Line of Marriage bends in a long curve down into the palm in the direction of Mars, it is in itself a sign of unhappiness in married life, but as a rule brought about by the quarrelsome jealous nature of the person *on whose hand it appears* (D, Fig. 45).

If such a line should end in an 'island', the marriage will end

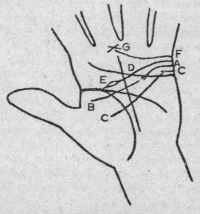

FIG. 45

in scandal or separation (E, Fig. 45). If, however, this line should end in a cross on the Mount of Mars, there is grave danger that the jealous nature of the subject will become dangerously out of control.

A similar indication is given if the Marriage Line ends in a distinct cross on the Mount of Saturn (F and G, Fig. 45). In this case the cause may not be jealousy, but the desire to remove the partner for some selfish purpose.

Such marks are still more accentuated if the Line of Heart is found curving downwards at its commencement to the Line of Head, as I have explained in the chapter on the Line of Heart.

When the Line of Marriage is itself clear and distinct, but with a series of little lines curving down from it, it indicates long years of ill-health for the partner of the person on whose hand the mark appears (A, Fig. 46).

If the Line of Marriage has an 'island' in it, it foretells trouble in the married life and some form of separation while the 'island' lasts (B, Fig. 46).

When this line seems full of a series of little 'islands', the subject should be warned not to marry as he or she is predestined to great unhappiness in married life.

When the Line of Marriage breaks into two parts and the upper part continues straight and clear, it indicates that a break will occur in the marriage, but that the subject is likely to remarry later the same partner (C, Fig. 46).

When the Line of Marriage goes to the Line of Sun or sends a branch line to the Mount of Sun, the person on whose hand this appears will marry someone of distinction or a person of exalted position.

When, on the contrary, the Line of Marriage curves downwards and cuts through the Line of Sun (D, Fig. 46), it indicates that the person on whose hand this mark appears will lose position by the marriage.

When a short strong line bars or cuts through the Line of Marriage, some great obstacle will arise to prevent marriage (E, Fig. 46).

When a fine line is seen above the Marriage Line, running

parallel with it, some deep affection will come into the person's life after marriage. This is likely to be confirmed if it is a serious affair by a second influence line to the Line of Fate above the one that tallies with the date of the principal marriage.

On all hands one is likely to find a Marriage Line on the Mount of Mercury, but it does not follow that all who have this mark marry. The line on the mount means that at some period of the life, as shown by the position of the line which I

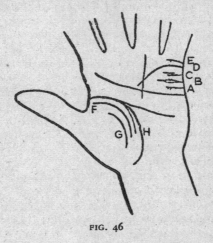

FIG. 46

have explained earlier, there arises a desire or longing in the man's or woman's nature to be married. If there is no other indication in the hand, the marriage will only be in *the mind of the subject*, and not an actuality.

This may sound difficult to understand, yet to those who study the lives of others, a climax or desire, such as I describe, comes sooner or later in the lives of every man or woman who are normal human beings.

I must now explain where another indication of marriage may be found, namely fine lines running parallel with the Line of Life on the Mount of Venus, and which are clear and distinct from the Line of Mars or double Line of Life. Taking

F, Fig. 46 to be the Line of Mars, G, Fig. 46 must be understood as another indication by which marriage or a union may be interpreted.

The Mars line in every case comes directly from the Mount of Mars, and denotes a strong robust vitality. It may also be taken as a double Line of Life, but the latter can also spring out of the Line of Life itself at any period during the run of life (H, Fig. 46).

Marriage lines on the Mount of Venus are also called 'Venus lines', and are usually only found on the hands of persons who have an intensely strong sex nature.

Now as 'sex appeal' varies so greatly in degree with the individual, these Venus lines must again be considered in connection with the type of hand on which they are found.

On a long refined type they represent the higher expression of the passionate nature, while on a short coarse type they represent the more animal or sensual.

Men or women with the Mount of Venus large or highly developed are more easily swayed by the gusts of passion that sweep through their lives.

On long narrow hands the Mount of Venus is naturally not so high or rounded, consequently a person of this class has more control over his or her passions. If such persons have many 'Venus lines', they may have equally as many love affairs, but from a more mental standpoint.

We will now return to the examination of the 'Venus lines' in themselves.

When a line which has been deep and strong appears to turn in on the mount away from the Line of Life, the person who has influenced the nature will cease to play any rôle, although the memory of the passionate love affair may remain (A, Fig. 47).

When a 'Venus line' appears with an island (B, Fig. 47), the person influencing the life will get into trouble and disgrace.

If a 'Venus line' crosses and joins with the Line of Life or sends a branch to it, the influence will become as strong as life itself (C, Fig. 47).

Should a 'Venus line' or a branch from it cross over and cut the Line of Fate, the influence thus indicated will cause injury to one's destiny (D, Fig. 47).

If the influence line or a branch from it cuts the Line of Sun, one's position or public reputation will be affected.

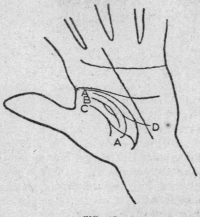

FIG. 47

I have now explained the three parts of the hand which have a bearing on the question of unions or marriages. It will be seen how important it is for the student to consider all these indications, and to take into account the class of hand on which these marks may be found.

## Chapter 22  Lines denoting children: the three bracelets

'How many children shall I have?' is a frequent question put to students of this science.

Owing to the accuracy I have been credited with on this subject, I have been requested by numerous readers of my other works to give still more information in writing this present book.

There are one or two points that must be considered before I explain the lines denoting children.

First, the student should examine what are called 'the bracelets', or those three lines that generally run parallel to one another on the wrist.

The first of these is the most important in deciding how many children are likely to be born.

The upper line nearest the palm (A, Fig. 48), the ancient Greeks in their study of the hand called the Bracelet of Venus. If this line was found rising in the form of an arch (A, Fig. 48), they forbade the woman to marry as they considered it was a sign of unusual suffering in child-birth, and if the arch formation was extreme, it indicated danger to the woman's life in the delivery of children.

In order to get as much information as was possible on such an important aspect of the subject, with considerable patience through many rebuffs, I finally got quite a number of doctors attending maternity hospitals in London and Paris to take notice of this line on the hands of patients who were admitted for confinement.

In almost every case of long protracted or difficult birth, they found that the Bracelet of Venus was a pronounced arch.

It was also noticed that the recovery after birth was much slower than in cases where the three bracelets were even or parallel with one another.

It is therefore necessary to consider the first bracelet, or, as the Greeks called it, 'the Bracelet of Venus', in estimating whether a woman is likely to have a large family or not. Apart from all questions of birth control or religious scruples, a woman who has suffered intensely, or who has been near to death in giving birth to her first child, will be less inclined to have children once she has passed through her first ordeal.

If the second bracelet is also arched like the first, the danger in child-birth is all the greater and the recovery still more protracted (B, Fig. 48).

When the third bracelet is formed like a series of little islands, or only half-way across the wrist, a considerable

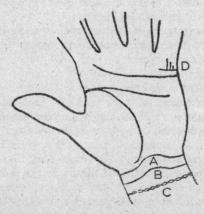

FIG. 48

amount of delicacy of the internal organs may be anticipated (C, Fig. 48).

When, however, the three bracelets are clear and distinct lying parallel to one another, a robust constitution is promised, provided of course that there are no bad indications given by the lines of Life and Health.

A woman with a long thin hand, with consequently the Mount of Venus under the base of the thumb narrow, will not be as likely to have as many children as a woman who has a broad type of hand with the Mount of Venus also broad.

A distinction must be made between a *broad* Mount of Venus and a *high* mount.

A woman with the latter formation is more amorous and sensual in her nature than a woman who has the mount broad. Intensely sensual, passionate people, it is well known, seldom have children. This point is then well worth attention in consideration of the question: 'How many children am I likely to have?'

The lines that indicate children are found as finely marked upright lines from the Line of Marriage on the Mount of Mercury (D, Fig. 48). The best plan to find these lines and to see which of them appears to be the most important is to gently press the surface of the mount where the Line of Marriage is found.

If out of three or four of these small lines we will say two appear to stand out clear and distinct, one will generally be found correct in stating that the woman will have two children that will live.

In some cases these lines indicating children may come up from the Heart Line through the Marriage Line. In such an instance the woman will be of such an affectionate disposition that she will be more bound up in her children than in any other part of her home life.

Strong or broad lines indicate males—fine lines, females.

If one of these lines appears more distinct than the others it will be found that the child indicated, be it the first, second or third, from *the outside of the hand*, will be the more prominent and successful provided the line appears straight and clear.

If one of these lines begins in an 'island' as it leaves the Marriage Line, delicacy of that child in its early years may be expected. If ending in an 'island' it foretells delicacy and likely death.

It is natural to suppose that some hands give greater details than others, as some people are more *mentally conscious* of everything that concerns them than are others.

It is not usual to find lines indicating children on men's hands. In some cases, however, they are found as clearly marked as on a woman's. This indicates that the man concerned will be exceptionally fond of children, and of deeply affectionate disposition.

The Girdle of Venus is that broken or unbroken line or series of lines like a semi-circle generally found rising between the first and second fingers and finishing between the third and fourth (A, Fig. 49).

It may also be found lying across the base of all the mounts under the fingers from the Mount of Jupiter to the Mount of Mercury, or it may be found terminating or running off the hand in, through or near the Line of Marriage.

In the first example (A), it is usually found associated with a highly strung intellectual disposition, a person unusually sensitive and swayed by moods.

As this mark is more generally found on a long narrow type of hand I do not ascribe to it the vicious sensuality that some writers make it appear to have. I agree with them, however, when this curious sign appears on a broad flabby sensual-looking hand, especially one when the Line of Head is seen curving downwards towards, or on the Mount of Luna (D, Fig. 49); such an indication with a large Mount of Venus will undoubtedly foreshadow vicious tendencies of a sensual and self-destructive character.

As I said before, the Girdle of Venus, whether broken or unbroken, is more usually found on a long narrow intellectual type, thus it is abnormal to find it on a broad fleshy hand and consequently if found denotes abnormal tendencies.

It must be remembered that short hands with stubby fingers belong to the more materialistic realm of life, while long hands with long fingers belong to a higher mental development.

The mounts of the palm in themselves express the qualities of the *mind*; it therefore follows that the Girdle of Venus lying across the mounts of the upper part of the hand must in itself have more a mental bearing than a physical one.

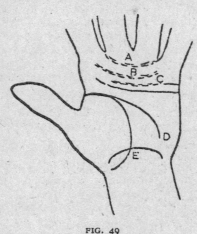

FIG. 49

When therefore not too much accentuated as in A, Fig. 49, it is not an unfavourable sign to have as it will give more sensitiveness to the artistic nature.

Such persons are capable of rising to great enthusiasm over anything that engages their mentality, but at the same time they will as easily descend to the lowest depths of depression if things do not go as they expect, or if they become disappointed by one of their idols falling off the pedestal on which they have placed them.

When the Girdle of Venus runs on to any part of the Mount of Jupiter (B, Fig. 49), such persons become hero-worshippers in every sense of the term, and in consequence suffer keenly through disillusionment.

If the Girdle of Venus passes off the hand through the Line of Marriage or near it (C, Fig. 49), married life will be marred by the highly sensitive and erotic nature of the person on whose hand this mark is found.

## The Via Lasciva

This line passes from the Mount of Luna into that of Venus (E, Fig. 49). It usually takes the form of a loop apparently joining the two mounts together. No matter what form it may take it is not a favourable mark to have. On a hard firm palm it will not have so much effect, but on a soft flabby hand, especially with Head Line curving downwards (see Plate 9), it indicates a lack of resistance to sensation and stimulation, especially to intoxicating liquors and such drugs as morphine, cocaine, hashish, etc., and is a warning for the exercise of will-power and abstinence.

On a hand with a straight Line of Head, the Via Lasciva considerably loses its meaning as if the mental will-power held its tendencies under restraint.

This strange mark is usually found on a hand which has at least some formation of the Girdle of Venus, but it can be found quite independent of it.

If the Via Lasciva should be noticed on the hand of a child or young person, every effort should be made to strengthen the will-power and warn them against self-indulgence of all kinds.

## The Ring of Saturn

The Ring of Saturn (A, Fig. 50) is a kind of semi-circle on the face of the Mount of Saturn. It is not often seen on hands and is a most unfortunate mark to find.

It appears to have a bearing on the mental outlook or character of the person on whose hand it may be found. Such persons are gloomy, melancholy and morose. They nurse imaginary grievances and cut themselves off from the society of their fellow beings.

They are usually unfortunate in everything they attempt, and if a sloping or weak-looking Head Line is found on the same hand, they are inclined to develop a decided tendency towards suicide.

This mark is more usually found when there is a heavily marked Line of Fate which runs up the hand to the Ring of

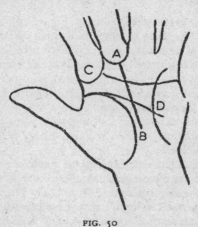

FIG. 50

Saturn. This solitary-looking Fate Line appears to intensify the isolated character indicated by the Ring of Saturn (B, Fig. 50).

I have seldom found a Line of Sun on such hands, nor have I ever seen a person with the Saturn influence, marked as I have described, successful in anything he has attempted.

## The Ring of Solomon

This mark is found on the Mount of Jupiter under the first finger. It is the complete reverse of the indications given by the Ring of Saturn, being in itself a sign of power and authority over others. It is usually formed as a kind of semi-circle on the face of the Mount of Jupiter (C, Fig. 50).

In ancient times the 'Ring of Jupiter' was considered a sign of occult power, and was called the 'Mark of the Master'. The qualities of Jupiter were designated to the Mount under the first finger because it is by the first finger one 'lays down the law to others'. By it man dictates to his fellow man, so it became the symbol of authority.

If therefore a Ring of Jupiter (or, as it is also called, 'The Ring of Solomon') is found on or around the mount, it appears to accentuate the qualities the mind represents and is consequently an excellent sign to possess.

This mark must not be confused with short straight lines like bars on the face of the Mount. Such bars indicate obstacles or barriers in the way of the attainment of the person's ambition.

Marks on the mounts will be fully explained in the chapter dealing with the mounts of the hand.

## The Line of Intuition

The Line of Intuition (D, Fig. 50), as a rule is only found on the philosophic, conic or psychic types of hands. It appears as a kind of semi-circle joining the Mounts of Mercury and Luna together. It denotes a highly strung, impressionable nature, one super-sensitive to surroundings, influences or the aura of other persons.

If this line is found on a hand its possessor will have clairvoyant gifts, presentiments, vivid dreams and perhaps visions. It is more often found on the psychic type of hand than any other.

In the illustrations given in the following chapters these marks are drawn with a fine geometrical precision in order to demonstrate the exact part of the hand on which they may be found, but of course they are never so exact.

It should be understood that all the minor marks should be clearly marked in the hand, even though uneven in shape.

Some hands show many of these lesser markings because the hand is covered with a multitude of lines running in all directions, and the criss-crossing of these lines form all kinds of patterns. In such a case the minor marks must lose their true significance to a certain extent.

The island is the splitting of a line, re-forming at either end, and can be small or large.

The star is usually uneven, and may be isolated or made up of small lines (forming a star shape) with a main line as part of the star. An example can be seen on the hand print of the Countess Hamon, under the Apollo finger on the Sun Line.

The cross is really a bar line cutting through either a main line or another short line. The Mystic Cross should be clearly marked between the Head and Heart lines, and stand alone even though the extremities may touch the Head and Heart Lines.

The square can be on a line or stand alone. It can be corner-wise, i.e. like a diamond, or can be two small lines joining two main lines.

The grille is seldom symmetrical, but is formed of several small lines criss-crossing.

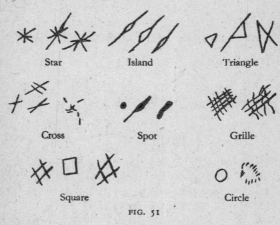

| Star | Island | Triangle |

| Cross | Spot | Grille |

| Square | Circle |

FIG. 51

The triangle can be a V shape attached to a main line, or a roughly defined triangle in a separate position or crossing another line.

All these signs must be boldly marked for true significance. Examples of formation are given in the illustration as a guide to the student.

L.O.

*The star* (Fig. 52) is often a sign of great importance, but its importance will be increased or diminished according to the place on the hand on which it is found.

On the upper part of the Mount of Jupiter (A, Fig. 52), if the Lines of Head, Fate and Sun are good, it is a magnificent promise of success in whatever the ambitions are centred on.

Lower down on the same mount it is also good, but indicates that the subject will be brought into contact with distinguished people and those of high authority in the world; more than that, the person himself will become great.

On the Mount of the Sun (B, Fig. 52), if touching or connected with a good Line of Sun, it promises unusual celebrity of the nature of fame and glory. It is also a sign of riches attained by the person through their success, but as a rule it does not promise happiness, for the subject has something in his or her disposition that will never be satisfied with anything attained.

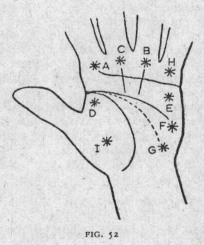

FIG. 52

On the centre of the Mount of Saturn (C, Fig. 52), it is a sign of some mysterious fatality that pursues the person all through his career.

It again singles out the man or woman for distinction, but one to be dreaded. It indicates that the possessor of this mark will be the plaything of fate, destined to be cast for strange rôles in life, but usually associated with tragedy. This is still more accentuated if a strong Line of Destiny touches this star.

On the Mount of Mars (positive) (D, Fig. 52), it promises distinction and celebrity from a military life, or as a leader in some revolutionary movement. On the opposite Mount of

Mars (negative), between the Lines of Head and Heart (E, Fig. 52), it shows that honour will be gained through patience and perseverance, by mental fighting as opposed to that of the physical.

On the Mount of Luna with a good Line of Head it promises brilliant success arising from the imaginative qualities such as invention if the Head Line is sloping, or in the domain of poetry, literature or art (F, Fig. 52).

With a very sloping or weak-looking Line of Head, and the star low down on the Mount (G, Fig. 52), the imagination will be inclined to run riot and may produce insanity.

As this star has often been found in this position on the hands of suicides, it has been considered by ancient writers to be a sign of drowning, but it may also be found on the hands of those who commit suicide by other means than water.

On the centre of the Mount of Mercury (H, Fig. 52), it denotes success in the qualities of the mind, especially in scientific pursuits. It is also a remarkable promise of distinction in a money-making career if the Line of Head lies straight or level across the hand underneath it.

On the Mount of Venus (I, Fig. 52), it denotes strong personal magnetism and success in love affairs.

## The cross

A cross if found standing out distinct by itself, and not formed by main lines crossing one another on the Mount of Jupiter, is the sign of love and affection for some person one may be proud of (A, Fig. 53).

When found near the commencement of the Line of Life it will be in the early years, on the centre of the mount in middle life, and down at the base or high up near the first finger late in life.

On the Mount of Saturn (B, Fig. 53), touching the Line of Fate, it usually denotes danger of violent death by accident, but if found standing out alone and distinct on this mount, it increases the fatalistic tendencies of the life.

On the Mount of the Sun it foreshadows disappointment in

the pursuit of fame or wealth, unless the Line of Sun proceeds beyond the cross, in which case it is temporary (C, Fig. 53).

A cross on the Mount of Mercury indicates a tendency towards duplicity (D, Fig. 53).

On the Mount of Luna with a sloping Head Line (E, Fig. 53), it denotes a fatal influence of the imagination. Persons with this mark deceive even themselves.

Low down towards the base of the Mount of Luna at the end of a voyage line it threatens danger from drowning (F, Fig. 53).

On the Mount of Venus when distinctly marked (G, Fig. 53), it indicates some great loss or trial of the affections of a passionate nature.

On the Mount of Mars positive, under Jupiter, it threatens violence and likely death in fighting. Many soldiers who lost their lives in the war of 1914–18 had this mark (H, Fig. 53).

On the Mount of Mars negative, under Mercury, the cross denotes the *mental* hostility of enemies (I, Fig. 53).

Above and slightly touching the Line of Head it fore-shadows a wound or accident to the head (J, Fig. 53).

If clear and distinct, touching the Line of Fate, it denotes trouble or opposition to one's career (K, Fig. 53).

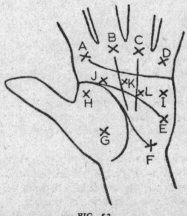

FIG. 53

By the side of the Line of Sun it threatens some loss or difficulty in one's success (L, Fig. 53).

## The square

What is called the square is one of the most interesting of the minor signs. It is generally designated as the 'Mark of Preservation'. It denotes that the man or woman will be protected or escape whatever danger is threatened at that particular period of the life (for dates see Chapter 25, on Time as Shown by the Hands).

When found on the Line of Life the person will escape the illness threatened at that period (A, Fig. 54). On the Line of Head it is a protection from accident to the head, and if it surrounds an 'island', from some brain malady (B, Fig. 54).

On the Line of Fate from loss or trouble at that date (C, Fig. 54).

On the Line of Sun generally preservation from scandal or attack on one's position (D, Fig. 54). On the Line of Health protection from some breakdown wherever the square may be found (E, Fig. 54).

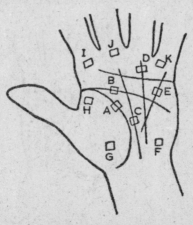

FIG. 54

On the Mount of Luna protection from dangers in voyages or travel (F, Fig. 54). On the Mount of Venus the subject will escape danger threatened by trouble brought on by the passionate nature (G, Fig. 54).

On the Mount of Mars (*positive*) it is a sign of preservation in fighting or in a military career (A, Fig. 54).

On the Mount of Jupiter protection in one's ambitions (I, Fig. 54). On Saturn preservation from fatalities (J, Fig. 54). On Mercury strength or protection from mental overstrain (K, Fig. 54).

The general rule to follow is that the square on any of the mounts protects the person from *the excess qualities of that particular mount*.

### The island

The 'island' can never be considered a fortunate sign. Its rôle is to break down or weaken the qualities of whatever line or mount of the palm on which it appears.

In the Line of Life it denotes illness or delicacy in the various parts of the body according to the position of the 'island' (A, Fig. 55). At the commencement of the Life Line a

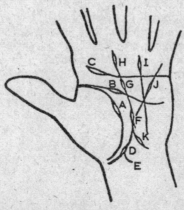

FIG. 55

series of 'islands' means delicacy in early life, which may be shown to be outgrown by the continuation of a strong, clear Life Line to the end. On the other hand the probable nature of the delicacy will be corroborated lower down on the Life Line if the tendencies towards illness increase as life goes on.

An 'island' high on the Life Line immediately following the span covering the early years relates to the upper part of the body and indicates that the lungs and bronchial tubes will be affected, *particularly if the nails are filberts* (see chapter on nails); lower down weakness of the digestive system, lower still the intestinal tract—still lower the kidneys, bladder and excretory organs.

In the Line of Head, mental weakness generally brought about by overstrain (B, Fig. 55).

An 'island' under the Mount of Jupiter indicating the danger of mental strain will most likely be due to over-ambition—under Saturn due to melancholia or shock; under the Mount of Sun, the eyes and frontal sinus above the eyes; under Mercury the fretful worrying state of the mind.

If the Heart Line commences with an 'island', hereditary heart disease is indicated, *especially if the nails are short with little or no moons* (C, Fig. 55).

Marked in the early years of the Fate Line, especially if that line appears to come from under the Mount of Venus (D, Fig. 55), the home life or family connections will trouble or injure the start of the career. If the Line of Fate should as well be connected with the Mount of Venus, the person will spoil or sacrifice his early years to some relation or for some reason in connection with his home life.

If a line of influence be found joining the 'island' some unfortunate love affair or early marriage will injure the man or woman in the early years of the career and prevent them from following their plans (E, Fig. 55).

An 'island' in what is called the Plain of Mars will foretell great difficulties at the date when the 'island' appears (F, Fig. 55).

If an 'island' is seen in the Line of Fate between the Head and Heart Lines in what is called the 'Quadrangle', the person will go through great mental trouble and anxiety in that period of his existence (G, Fig. 55).

An 'island' at the end of the Line of Fate (H, Fig. 55) is a terrible sign of loss and misfortune in the closing years of the career.

An 'island' at the end of the Line of Sun means that the career, no matter how brilliant it has been, will end in calumny and loss (I, Fig. 55).

An 'island' in the Health Line will cause grave danger to the health and increase whatever illness or disease may be indicated elsewhere by the hand (J, Fig. 55).

An 'island' on a line of influence joining the Fate Line shows there is some trouble or scandal connected with the person who influences or joins one's fate (K, Fig. 55).

An 'island' on any mount weakens the particular qualities of the mount or part of the hand on which it is found.

### The circle

The circle is somewhat similar in its meaning to the 'island', but not as important. It generally appears in a series of small lines or dots. Its only favourable indication is when it is found with a good Line of Sun on the mount of that name (A, Fig. 56), for the reason that here it becomes the symbol of the sun itself.

On any other line it weakens the power of that line. On the base of the Mount of Luna any form of the circle indicates danger from water, or travel (B, Fig. 56).

### The spot

What is called the 'spot', dent or hole in any line indicates the temporary cessation of the activities of that line at that particular moment. It is more often found on the Lines of Life, Head and Health than on any other part of the hand.

On the Line of Life it is the indication of a sudden sharp attack of illness (C, Fig. 56). On the Line of Head it usually foretells a severe blow or concussion of the brain (D, Fig. 56).

## The trident

This mark is so called from the fact that it appears as its name implies, namely in the form of a three-pronged trident. It is not often found, but when it is, it is considered an excellent mark to possess. On the Mount of Jupiter it foretells success in ambition (E, Fig. 56)—on the Mount of the Sun, power through wealth.

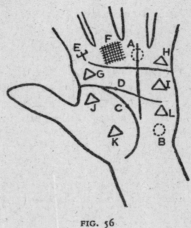

FIG. 56

## The grille

This mark is quite often met with on the Mounts of the Hand. It denotes confusion of ideas, lack of continuity of purpose in relation to the *qualities of the particular mount on which it appears.* On the Mount of Jupiter it denotes egotism, pride of power, but that of a self-willed person who will attempt too many things in order to satisfy his or her ambition.

It is a specially bad sign when found on the Mount of Saturn, as it indicates the breaking up of the Fate Line into a multiplicity of wasted effort, with no fixed purpose in the individual's life (F, Fig. 56). In character on this mount it denotes a morbid tendency with an undercurrent of extreme selfishness. On the Mount of the Sun it indicates that the person will be inclined to gratify vanity by committing folly of every description in their desire for celebrity.

## The triangle

This mark is often found very clear and distinct. It should not be confused with the chance crossing of lines with each other.

It is exceptionally good when found on any part of the Mount of Jupiter. It promises more than average success in organisation, in the management of people, in the handling of masses, in dictating to others and success in Government or political life (G, Fig. 56).

On the Mount of Saturn it denotes talent and power for research into hidden things, also for the use of occult powers or the unusual in scientific work.

On the Mount of the Sun it denotes the practical application of art and a calm demeanour as regards one's fame or success in life. Even without any very definite Line of Sun a well-marked Triangle on the mount of that name is an excellent promise of success if there is a good Line of Head.

On the Mount of Mercury it balances the mental qualities and strengthens the talents indicated (H, Fig. 56).

On the Mount of Mars under Mercury, the Triangle gives to it increased mental activity (I, Fig. 56).

On the Mount of Mars under Jupiter it denotes sciences in fighting or warfare, and like the square it is also a sign of protection and of presence of mind in danger (J, Fig. 56).

On the Mount of Venus it gives reason, method and restraint in affairs of passion (K. Fig. 56).

On the Mount of Luna it gives balance and judgment to the imagination (L, Fig. 56).

## The Mystic Cross

The Mystic Cross, or as it is called, La Croix Mystique, is found in the centre of what is termed 'The Quadrangle', or in the upper or lower end of it between the Lines of Head and Heart.

It may also be formed by a line from the Head to the Heart across the Line of Fate. It denotes gifts of mysticism and an intense love of occultism.

When high up almost under Jupiter it denotes the desire for and use of occult powers in connection with the person's ambitions (A, Fig. 57). When apparently more connected with the Line of Heart, it gives a more superstitious nature, especially if the Line of Head under it is sloping towards the Mount

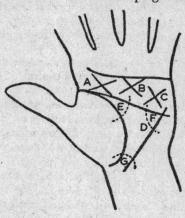

FIG. 57

of Luna (B, Fig. 57). The length of the Line of Head must be considered with this mark. A short line will naturally be inclined to be more superstitious than a long formation across the hand.

When nearer the wider end of the Quadrangle, to study or desire to penetrate the mysteries of occultism will only be apparent as interest taken in such things (C, Fig. 57).

When formed by a line from the Line of Head crossing the Fate under the Mount of Saturn, the pursuit of occultism will influence the entire destiny (see the hand of 'Cheiro', Plate 5).

If the Line of Head appears to rise upward under the Mystic Cross at any point, the person will become a serious mental student of all subjects dealing with occultism. This also denotes quick keen intuition about the people one meets.

## The quadrangle

The quadrangle is that space that lies between the Lines of Heart and Head. When this space appears even and well shaped, it is a sign of balanced judgment which is to be expected on account of the Line of Head being level.

If the Line of Heart is seen bending down into the quadrangle, it denotes that the affections will more or less interfere with the judgment.

If the Line of Head bends upwards and narrows the quadrangle the person will be more practical in affairs of the heart.

It is not a good sign to have the quadrangle filled with a lot of meaningless lines. The *cleaner it is the better*, with the exception, of course, of the main lines of the palm that pass through it on their way to the different mounts.

## The Great Triangle

What is called the 'Great Triangle' is formed by the Lines of Life, Head and Health (D, Fig. 57). The larger the formation of the triangle the better, for the reason that when large, the Line of Health does not touch and cut off the Line of Life. Also for the very important reason that to have a really large triangle, the Line of Head must be straight across the hand.

It has therefore been laid down as a rule in this study that the larger the 'Great Triangle' is, the better it must be for the person on whose hand it may be found.

## The upper angle

The upper angle (E, Fig. 57) which is formed by the Lines of

Head and Life should be clearly defined in shape. If too acute the person would have the Line of Head too low down for it to be a good sign of mentality.

If, on the contrary, this angle is open, the person will be inclined to suffer from lack of caution, and dash into dangerous hazards or take chances with life. If not *too* wide, this larger angle is an excellent sign on the hand of an actor or actress, or those who lead any form of public life. It denotes a keen sense of drama or the dramatic instinct, and with a good Line of Head gives freedom of thought and originality.

## The middle angle

The middle angle is formed by the Lines of Head and Health (F, Fig. 57). A wide angle in this position is better than an acute one, for the reason that it shows that the Line of Head is more level.

If acute, it would not only make a more sloping Head Line, but it would bring the Line of Health more sharply across the palm towards the life and so indicate more likelihood of delicacy.

The same rule applies to the lower angle (G, Fig. 57). If acute it would bring the Health Line too close to the Line of Life.

## Travel, voyages and accidents

Travel, voyages and accidents caused by such things are shown in two ways. By lines on the Mount of Luna that lie horizontally on this mount, and by lines that descend from the Line of Life and go more or less outwards in the direction of the Mount of Luna. The latter are the more important of the two kinds.

Still another indication, but very different in character, is when the Life Line divides with one branch going out towards the Mount of Luna (A, Fig. 58), while the other continues round the base of the Mount of Venus (B, Fig. 58), illustrates a complete change from one country to another. If this outer line is more heavily marked or looks more important than B continuing round the Mount of Venus, it promises long residence in a country far from that of birth.

Should the two lines A and B appear equally strong, it indicates long and continuous voyages to and from the two places.

If the line to B should fade out, as it may do after a few years, then the person will settle permanently in some far-off country.

If the Line of Life itself should leave its usual position and go across or towards the Mount of Luna, the change of place

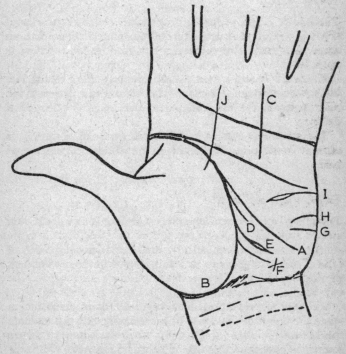

FIG. 58. TRAVEL, VOYAGES AND ACCIDENTS

or country will be all the more decided, as if the person had it written in his destiny from the time of birth that he would change from his own land and go to another.

A very remarkable point is one I have proved by long experience, that if at the same date in the age of the person the Line of Sun is good (C, Fig. 58), the change will be a successful one. If, however, the Line of Sun looks weak at that date, or fades out, then the change to another country will be unfortunate.

The same rule applies when the entire Life Line leaves its usual position and goes outward towards the Mount of Luna. The indication of success or failure will be still more accentuated should the Fate Line as well as the Sun Line look weak, or fade out from the date of the change.

This information gathered from my own experience has not to my knowledge been given to the world before.

Fine downward lines that leave the outside of the Life Line also denote voyages or long journeys (D, Fig. 58). If one of the lines of travel runs into an 'island' the journey will end badly—generally in relation to the defeat of one's plans (E, Fig. 58).

Should, however, a cross, no matter how small, be seen close to the 'island', or at the end of the travel line, it foreshadows danger (F, Fig. 58).

Travel lines are also shown lying across the face of the Mount of Luna (G, Fig. 58).

When these travel lines curve downwards (H, Fig. 58), they are not as favourable as when lying straight across the Mount of Luna.

If the line ends in an 'island' or has one towards the end of it, the travel or journey will end in loss or disappointment (I, Fig. 58).

I have given examples of how accidents are shown in connection with travel. There is, however, another sign of danger or accident, but one that may be caused by any form of fatality. This is when a line is seen coming from the Mount of Saturn and cutting the Life Line at any point (J, Fig. 58).

This line from Saturn can easily be distinguished from a line that rises *from* the Line of Life towards Saturn, as I have described in Chapter 16 relating to the Life Line. The line of fatality from Saturn it will be seen cuts *through* the Line of Life, threatening danger where the two lines intersect.

## *Chapter 25*    Time and dates of events as shown by the hand

Time—or how to tell when changes or events took place or are about to take place in a person's life—is one of the most interesting points in this study.

As the ancient Greeks in their study of the hand considered the age of twenty-one to be man's entry into the battle of life, I place this year at the outside edge of what is called 'the Plain of Mars'. The period from the age of twenty-one to thirty-five is generally the critical period in the struggle for existence. It is in reality the foundation on which man builds for the following thirty-five years (Fig. 59).

If he has not by the middle of his life done something to warrant his existence, it is not to be expected that he would make much out of the remaining half.

In reading hands this must be considered as more or less a crucial period. If from this time on the Lines of Fate or Sun, or both, are apparently getting weaker, it indicates that the man or woman has spent their forces and in a sense is going 'downhill'.

On the contrary, should these lines appear stronger from this centre point, the signification is that the person has made good in the battle of life, and the tide of fate is with him in his onward stride.

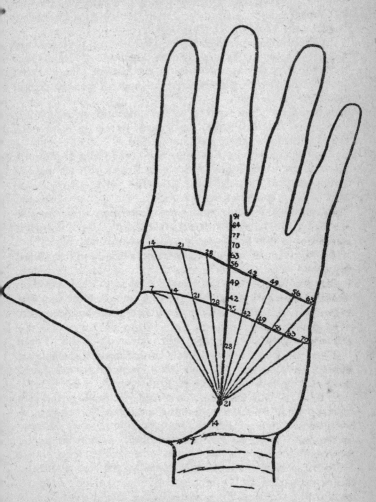

FIG. 59. TIME AND DATES OF EVENTS

For dates of events on the Line of Life such as illness, change of place and such like, it is more logical to assume that the rays of influence descend from the Mount of Mercury (the mind) towards the Line of Life (Fig. 60).

It will be remembered that when dealing with the subject of health (Chapter 18), I pointed out that the Line of Health came from Mercury downwards towards the Line of Life, and that where these two lines intersected one another was the critical point for life or death.

It is as if the mind acted on by the subconscious brain knew in advance or felt the germs of disease that are the enemies of the vitality and so affect the Line of Life.

To all those who have this line from the Mount of Mercury towards the Line of Life, I can give this word of hope and encouragement, namely, there is no line on the hand *that is more subject to change and improvement* than is the Line of Health.

Impressions of hands taken a few years apart will show this line to be on the increase or the reverse. I have even known it to fade out altogether as the subject controlled his or her worrying disposition and took things from a philosophical standpoint.

In considering the date of a breakdown or illness marked on the Line of Life, it is necessary to look across to the opposite side of the hand and note the condition or appearance of the Line of Health.

If at the same date where a sign such as an 'island' is seen in the Line of Life and opposite to it the Health Line appears heavily marked or also with an 'island' in it, the illness will be more serious and recovery from it more protracted.

The nature of the illness at the date indicated on the Life Line has to be determined by an examination of the various parts of the hand as I have explained fully, earlier in these pages. It is most important also to observe the nails on the fingers as they give details about inherited tendencies that cannot be obtained by any other means. (See chapter on the nails.)

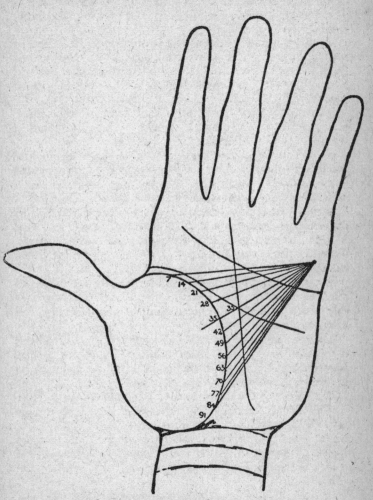

FIG. 60. DATES OF EVENTS ON THE LINE OF LIFE

*Part 3*  Some Famous Hands

## *Chapter 26* Interesting and famous hands

Having received so many requests from all parts of the world that I would analyse or point out the most important characteristics of some interesting as well as famous persons' hands, it gives me pleasure to take this opportunity of doing so.

It would not be right to go into the private lives of those who in consulting me gave me impressions of their hands for my collection. I will consequently only call attention to the salient points in the characters or careers of those whose right hands appear in this part of the book.

As the right hand shows the active or developed side of the individual, it is in consequence the only one I have the right to publish.

Knowing what an enormous help it will be to students of the subject to have before them impressions of real hands, I take this opportunity of expressing my thanks to all who have made this possible.

I have had to strictly limit my selection to hands that have some distinct feature described in these pages.

As my collection to date is upwards of 60,000 impressions, it will be understood that it would be impossible to publish a representative selection of such a number without making this volume too large for publication.

I take this opportunity of thanking Olga Hall-Brown for the beautifully simple way she has made the drawings of hands and lines to illustrate my words. In order to make her diagrams express exactly what every mark is intended to mean, she laid aside every other claim on her time to master the study of hands under my tuition, so that her drawings would have an accuracy not to be obtained by any other means.

In conclusion I would like to impress on the minds of parents and guardians of young people the value of this study in enabling them to see in advance the tendencies for good or evil in the hands of those whose destiny is theirs to guide.

This study of life by means of the hand is not a difficult one to the person who has a little patience to grasp its fundamental rules, and there is no study in the world that gives a greater reward.

To be able to read character alone is helpful to all, but to be able to look far into the future and aid others by counsel and advice is something so nearly divine that the recompense this study gives is beyond all price.

In this chapter I will diverge from examples of famous people and explain the accompanying impression of the right hand of a man showing some unusual and extraordinary lines.

As this man is still living and today occupying a successful and important position, I must exercise my privilege of withholding his name on account of certain eventful periods in his past career.

It will be noticed that there is one straight line lying across the hand from side to side (Plate 10). This is the Line of Head and Heart combined, which I have fully described when dealing with the Line of Head.

The line above this peculiar and unusual mark is the Girdle of Venus, which runs off the palm in the direction of the Marriage Lines.

In dealing with this peculiar Line of Head I have stated 'a long straight Line of Head going directly from one side of the hand to the other denotes that the subjec thas more than ordinary intellectual power, and more especially so if at its source it rises independently of the Line of Life'.

In speaking of the Girdle of Venus I said: 'If the Girdle of Venus passes off the hand through or near the Line of Marriage, married life will be marred by the highly sensitive **erotic nature** of the person on whose hand this mark is found.'

In writing of the Line of Fate, I said: 'When lying very close to the Life Line, home surroundings and ties of relationship have stood in the way, and the subject has been sacrificed in the early years to the wishes of others.'

I have also stated that if the Fate Line is stopped by the Line of Head, some mental action will injure the destiny, or it will be thwarted by the person's own mentality.'

All these indications may be seen on the accompanying impression. The history of the man is as follows:

He was held back by home surroundings in his early years, his people being too poor to give him anything more than an ordinary education. (Note the commencement of the Line of Fate.) At twelve years of age his father died, and until twenty-one he was the sole support of his mother who was a confirmed invalid.

He first sold papers in the streets of Chicago, then became a messenger boy in a shipping office and got a good position in this business in his twenty-first year. Note his Fate Line bending outwards into the palm.

At twenty-five he married a rich woman. Note strong influence line joining the Fate at this period. From then on to thirty he had phenomenal success in business, becoming sole owner of the shipping company, and organiser of a large transportation service. (Note strengthening of the Fate Line after influence line joins it.)

Requiring more capital he sold large blocks of stock in his company which, through the actions of a dishonest secretary in falsifying the books, were utterly valueless.

At the same period in his career his wife left him for another man. Strangely enough this man became his most vindictive enemy. (Note Line of Opposition across the Line of Fate.) He obtained information through the wife of the fraudulent issue of stock and disclosed same to the public prosecutor, who sent the owner of this hand to prison for a term of three years. (Note complete gap or cessation of the first Line of Fate at about this period of his career.)

While serving his sentence he planned out another large business scheme, which on leaving prison he brought into execution, and was again successful. (Note new outer Fate Line commencing while he was in prison.)

Observe that both Fate Lines inclining towards Jupiter, the Mount of Ambition, are stopped by the Line of Head in or about his fortieth year. Here this man met 'his Waterloo' in a colossal mental blunder in speculation by which he lost a fortune.

Another Fate Line has, however, already commenced, but one of a different character from the others. This new one is in the centre of the palm, has no longer the intensely ambitious indications of the others, but its course instead is directed towards the base of the second finger—that of Saturn.

A decidedly strong Line of Sun now appears promising wealth, position and honour for the rest of the career, while the Line of Fate high up under the second finger is again turning towards the ambitious Mount of Jupiter.

This man occupies a position of weight and authority in the world of finance such as few men have ever attained.

His Line of Life is extremely long. The Line of Health is barely marked and does not attack the life at any period.

He only married once—his one experience being enough.

*Chapter 28*    The Rt. Hon. William Ewart Gladstone

Mr. Gladstone gave me an autographed impression of his hand about a year before he died. He invited me to Hawarden Castle, and at the end of the interview gave me the remarkable impression of his hand (Plate 11) which is the only one in existence.

His hand bears out the truth of this study in no uncertain manner. The Line of Head is unusually long, crossing the palm from one side to the other—a sign of exceptional mentality and brain power.

It will be remembered that this remarkable man was one of the greatest mathematicians of his day, he was several times Chancellor of the Exchequer, and produced some of the most remarkable Budgets in the history of British government. He was also four times Prime Minister of England.

In his private life he was a great scholar, an authority on ancient Greek and Hebrew, and in his seventy-eighth year he mastered the Basque language—one of the most difficult in Europe.

The fine lines rising up from the Head Line under the base of the first finger denote the mental ability to dictate to others, while the extreme length of this Line of Head slightly sloping downwards indicates eloquence and the gift of expression which was one of the great characteristics of Gladstone's brilliant career in the House of Commons.

The Line of Fate or Destiny may be seen rising from the wrist and terminating in several very distinct branches, two turning towards the base of the first finger, two terminating under the second finger and one proceeding across the base of the third. This is very unusual and denotes strong individuality, and by turning towards the third finger the Mount of Sun denotes remarkable glory and success in public life.

As I stated in the chapter dealing with the Line of Sun, any clear straight line found rising up to the base of the third finger on a hand with a good Line of Head is always a promise of distinction and success.

In the case of Gladstone not only may the Line of Destiny be seen sending one of its branches towards the third finger, but there are also very distinct lines running upwards through the palm towards this position.

What is called the 'double Line of Life' is also shown in this impression. This denotes unusual vitality and a robust constitution, and is the promise not only of length of life, but excellent health till the end. It will be remembered that Gladstone pursued his favourite exercise of cutting down trees up to a few months before his last illness.

His hand also contains the rare and unusual Line of Intuition very strongly and clearly marked.

The type of the hand is that of the philosophic with an exceptionally long fourth finger, in itself denoting eloquence and mental grasp of subjects that the long Line of Head under it may become engaged in.

With the passing of Gladstone, England lost her greatest statesman.

*Chapter 29*  Count John MacCormack, the Irish tenor

The hand of this celebrated man should be of great interest to the general public as well as to the student of this study (Plate 12).

It will be noticed that the Line of Head is long and level, bearing out my remarks dealing with the hands of musicians when speaking of the Line of Head in an earlier part of this book, descriptive of the square hand with conic fingers. Dealing with this, I wrote: 'This blend of two opposite types, curiously as it might appear at first sight, produces the class of disposition that can excel in music or in composition of music. The logical reason for this being that the square hand in itself represents practicality and level-headedness—a balance necessary for the emotional, artistic temperament of the musician or composer.'

The rounded conic fingers in John MacCormack's case denote the supremely artistic emotional nature, but held under control and well directed by the indications of the long, level Line of Head.

The Line of Sun on this hand also bears out in a remarkable manner my description of it in Chapter 20. It may be seen rising upward from the Line of Fate at a date in the career corresponding to about twenty-eight years of age. It was just about this period that this justly celebrated artist and singer became universally acclaimed as one of the greatest tenors the world has ever known.

The only bad indication on this hand is that of the Line of Health from under the fourth finger passing downward across the palm in opposition to the Line of Life. Although John MacCormack was a man of magnificent physique, the strength of the Health Line shows the strain on his nervous system caused by the exigencies of his career.

The hand of this celebrated singer is an interesting study (Plate 13). In her very early years everything appeared against her (note Line of Fate rising from the Mount of Venus and Line of Head tied closely to that of Life, then forcing its way out and crossing the entire palm).

Madame Nordica was born at Farmington, Maine, on December 12th, 1859, and began her study of music there which she completed in Italy after a hard struggle.

She made her début at the Covent Garden Opera House in 1887, singing the rôle of Brescia in 'La Traviata' at a moment's notice. She was then in her twenty-eighth year. (Note Line of Sun appearing at that date.) After this she went forward to fame and fortune.

At the age of thirty-seven (note change in Line of Fate), she returned to the United States, March 1896), making a pronounced success at the Metropolitan Opera House in New York.

Madame Nordica, although being endowed with a beautiful soprano voice, acknowledged that her great success was due to hard mental work. She sang in Italian, German and French as well as English, and she had no less than fifty grand opera rôles in her repertoire, her greatest successes being in difficult Wagnerian parts.

For many years she suffered considerably internally (see long island in Line of Life). She died on May 10th, 1914, from pneumonia brought on by her terrible experience in the shipwreck of the *Tasman* in the Gulf of Papua. She was then in her fifty-fifth year. (Note Line of Life cut by Health Line coming from two islands that have almost the shape of lungs. Also note voyage line pointing towards a cross on the Mount of Luna.)

An interesting minor mark which is to be seen on this hand is the Line of Intuition lying as a semi-circle from Mercury to Luna—a mark very rarely found.

The type of hand is square with conic rounded fingers.

Madame Nordica was married three times. Her first husband was Mr. F. A. Gower of the Gower-Bell Telephone fame. This marriage was not a happy one and its ending was peculiar. Her husband attempted to cross the Straits of Dover in a balloon and was never heard of again. Madame Nordica had to wait seven years before the Courts presumed his death.

In 1896 she married Herr Dormë, an Austrian tenor. This was also unhappy and ended in separation and divorce.

Her third marriage was with Mr. George W. Young, an American banker who survived her.

Madame Nordica was extremely lovable and good-hearted, but not demonstrative or showy in her affections. She helped many young singers to realise their ambition for a musical career, but she never allowed the good she did to be advertised in the Press.

*The hands of Lillian Nordica and
Count John MacCormack*

Cheiro has, of course, given his analysis of these hands in the accompanying histories, but it is fascinating to note the similarities in the hands of these famous artists. The student may find it of great interest to examine these similarities more closely because both artists achieved the highest fame as singers. In fact, the hands might almost be those of brother and sister. For a quick appraisal I give below the main points for comparison.

Both hands have square palms with pronounced Venus mounts, long straight Head Lines and good Mercury fingers, denoting physical vitality, love of music and melody, lively mentality, excellent powers of concentration and logical thinking.

The conic fingers on both hands add intuition, impulse, artistic appreciation and quick reactions to future possibilities. The fingers have padded basal phalanges showing an appreciation of material values, but the mentality always in control.

Both Heart Lines show warmth of emotion combined with idealism, and the Luna mounts are strong, adding to the imaginative expression. The outer edges of both palms have a full curve, indicating a certain creative ability, all very necessary for artistic expression.

Note also the straight setting of the fingers on the palms, and the spaces between the fingers together with the angle at which the thumbs are held. These show self-confidence, and the desire to live their lives with independence of thought and action so as to express their personalities, both in their own way.

L.O.

*Chapter 31*   The Rt. Hon. Joseph Chamberlain
and his son Sir Austen—an example of heredity as
shown by the lines on the hand

On the morning of 23rd June, 1894, I called at the House of
Commons to keep an appointment made for me by Mr. Joseph
Chamberlain. I showed him the impression I had just taken of
the right hand of his son, Austen Chamberlain, and found that
my theory of heredity as shown by the lines on the hand
interested him deeply.

When these two right hands of father and son are compared
(Plate 14) it will be seen that the principal lines are exactly
similar to one another.

'So you say,' he remarked, reflectively, 'it means that my
son, Austen, will have a career in every way like my own. He
has entered Parliament only two years ago, having been
returned by East Worcestershire in 1892.'

'Yes,' I answered, 'he will even occupy positions in parlia-
mentary life as you have filled, but he will not reach the zenith
of his career until 1925. In that year I would predict he will
have some great international triumph and have some great
honour conferred on him.'*

The student will notice that the Line of Head on both these
hands occupies an exactly similar position. The Line of Fate,

* After the International Peace Conference in 1925 he received knight-
hood.

although not so strong on the hand of the son, yet follows a like position as that on the hand of his father.

The Line of Health from the Mount of Mercury on the palm of the son is, fortunately for him, not as pronounced as the same line on Mr. Joseph Chamberlain's hand. It will be remembered that Mr. Joseph Chamberlain was afflicted by paralysis towards the closing years of his life, while Sir Austen himself had an extreme nervous breakdown after the strain of going through the Peace Conference and had to retire for some time from public life.

These hands of a distinguished father and an equally distinguished son are a remarkable example of heredity as shown by the lines on the hand.

I refer the reader back to Part II dealing with travel lines and indications of death by accidents. It will be noticed in this case (Plate 15) that the Line of Head is, towards the end, divided into two very distinct branches   the upper end lying perfectly straight and slightly turning upward, the lower sloping towards the Mount of Luna.

This indication denotes a contradiction in the nature   the upper line being decidedly level-headed and practical befitting his career as a soldier and organiser—the lower showing the other side of his mental disposition inclined to artistic and imaginative pursuits, all the more emphasised by the fact of his hand being unusually long with rather philosophic knotty fingers.

This latter side of his character he exercised in his private life, being a profound student of literature and languages and a connoisseur of such things as Chinese and Oriental porcelains. It is also not generally known by the public, who thought of him only as a great soldier, that Lord Kitchener was devoted to music and passed many hours of whatever leisure time he had playing both on the piano and on a reed instrument he learned during his life among the Arabs in Egypt, and which he played equal to any native.

The Line of Head being so closely joined at its beginning to the Line of Life indicates an extremely sensitive nature, especially emphasised by its being on such a long-shaped hand. The straight lines rising upward from the commencement of the Head Line on the Mount of Jupiter under the first finger, however, indicates power of command over others—a nature that could conquer its sensitiveness and dictate or 'lay down the law', if placed in any position of authority.

The Line of Heart shows an affectionate but undemonstrative nature and, with part of it drooping downward to join the Line of Head, indicates disappointment in the affections which, perhaps, accounted for his never marrying.

The Line of Sun or Success, as will be noticed, is remarkably good on Lord Kitchener's hand, while the Line of Fate sends off branch lines towards the first finger. The Line of Life gave the expectation of a long life under ordinary conditions, but my prediction that Lord Kitchener's life would end in his sixty-sixth year, by disaster at sea, was based on the cross at the end of the travel line opposite the age of sixty-six, when the disaster to H.M.S. *Hampshire* took place. (The line of travel and cross are fairly distinct in the reproduction of the impression of the hand.)

I made this prediction at my interview with him at the War Office on the 21st July, 1894, the date on which I took the impression reproduced in these pages. Lord Kitchener was then in his forty-fourth year.

## *Chapter 33*   Mata Hari

The reproduction (Plate 16) of the right hand of Mata Hari, the famous woman spy, is taken from the impression I made of her hand in Paris. It is initialled by her: 'M. H., Paris, 1900', just seventeen years before her execution in the prison of Vincennes.

The full account of my meeting with this remarkable woman is related in my autobiography.

The principal points of interest to the student in studying this hand are the following:

The wide space that may be noticed between the Lines of Life and Head, under the base of the first finger, the indication of a strongly dramatic temperament.

The Line of Head itself, with two long branches from it, the lower indicating a romantic, highly imaginative disposition; the upper, practicality, with unusual mental will-power. Three lines of Fate going to the Mount of Saturn, indicating what is called a 'double life'.

The Line of Health, from the base of the fourth finger, showing the ever-increasing nervous tension of the life led.

The Line of Sun, which, at the commencement, promised success in a public career, fading out about the centre of the palm, just about the part where a double Fate Line appears;

and the 'Lines of Marriage or Unions' all bending downward on the Mount of Mercury.

One of the most remarkable signs on the hand of Mata Hari is that one of the lines of Fate (or line of Saturn, as it may also be called) forms a triangle with the line from Mars to Saturn and may be seen cutting through the Line of Life at about her thirty-seventh year—the fatal year of her life.

The type of hand is that of the conic or artistic, with the contradictory indication of the upper Line of Head being straight and level.

*Chapter 34*   Erich von Stroheim, film actor and director

The impression of this hand is another remarkable example of the truth that underlies this study (Plate 17).

One cannot help but remark the position of the Line of Head with the space between it and the Line of Life at the commencement, the indication of natural dramatic instinct; while at its termination it has a forked formation denoting originality and inventive faculties.

The Line of Life is clear and long with an inner line coming from it showing strong vitality and robustness of the constitution.

The Line of Health, it will be noticed, although heavily marked on the opposite side of the hand, fails to approach or cut through the Line of Life—an excellent promise of good health in late years.

The Line of Fate so widely separate from that of Life shows there were no family ties to hold him back at the commencement of his career. This class of Fate Line also indicates strong individuality of an independent nature that could stand little or no control by others.

The Line of Sun to the third finger begins about the twenty-eighth year, and is remarkably well marked from then onwards.

It will be noticed that the Line of Fate or Destiny appears

to be stopped or arrested by the Head Line at a little past the centre of the career.

At about this period Erich von Stroheim made the mental mistake of producing pictures at such enormous expense that financial backers turned against him, one critic making the caustic if exaggerated remark that the snowflakes in one of his productions 'cost a thousand dollars each!' (Note the line of enmity and opposition across the Fate Line at this period.)

Shortly after the change shown in the centre of the hand, it will be noticed that a new Line of Fate appears, and with the excellent Line of Sun continuing to the base of the third finger, there is no doubt that Erich von Stroheim's remarkable talents will in the end gain for him renewed recognition and success in the world of pictures.

## *Chapter 35*    Countess Hamon

Countess Hamon's hand is peculiarly interesting to the student. It is a perfect example of a pure conic type, but with a straight Line of Head (Plate 18).

When describing the conic or artistic hand, I explained that it is normal to find on it a sloping Head Line, and therefore when a straight line was found its meaning would be strongly emphasised.

In Countess Hamon's case the conic shape gives her the artistic nature with its love of colour, beautiful surroundings and versatility in the direction of art in all its various forms.

In her early years she gave great promise as a singer, but the condition of her health cut short her musical career, her throat becoming injured by an attack of diphtheria, which completely ruined her voice and altered her destiny.

She then turned her artistic desires to painting, and did some remarkable work in crayons, using the sensitive tips of her fingers instead of the ordinary method. Ill-health as indicated by the long island on the inside or Double Life Line prevented her again making headway. To regain her health she travelled extensively, finally arriving in Egypt. Here the atmosphere, the colour and the glamour captured her artistic imagination and satisfied her innate desire for beauty. She left civilisation as she knew it and for a period of about five years lived in a caravan in the Sahara Desert.

Returning in her twenty-eighth year to England (see normal Fate Line commencing in the centre of the palm about this age), she re-entered social life.

From this time onward her straight Head Line dominated her artistic nature and developed it on practical and resourceful lines. Such studies as chemistry, botany, entomology and tropical agriculture have since occupied her time—unusual studies for a woman, but quite in keeping with the straight Line of Head on the conic hand.

In her thirty-fifth year she married for the second time. (See line of influence joining Fate Line at this date.) It will be seen that her first marriage was not successful by the drooping curved lines from the Line of Heart and on the Mount of Mercury.

From the middle of the life onward there are three Lines of Fate in this hand, one from the Line of Life that goes right on to Saturn slightly bending towards the Mount of Sun, a centre one which relates to her home life, and a third which relates to the unusual career she has made her own. The latter by its depth and strength promises to become the dominant fate, and by its inclination towards the Mount of Jupiter backed up by a strong Line of Sun indicates success and distinction in the work it represents.

In following up these indications of success, it is interesting to note that the Countess Hamon has twice been recognised by Governments, having been decorated by the King of Spain and by the Khedive of Egypt. Note the star formation on the end of the Sun Line under Apollo.

The Health Line is not a favourable one, indicating a highly strung nervous temperament in itself, and giving further warning of trouble by running towards an island low down on the Line of Life.

# Index

All Sphere Books are available at your bookshop or newsagent, or can be ordered from the following address: Sphere Books, Cash Sales Department, P.O. Box 11, Falmouth, Cornwall.

Please send cheque or postal order (no currency), and allow 19p for postage and packing for the first book plus 9p per copy for each additional book ordered up to a maximum charge of 73p in U.K.

Customers in Eire and B.F.P.O. please allow 19p for postage and packing for the first book plus 9p per copy for the next 6 books, thereafter 3p per book.

Overseas customers please allow 20p for postage and packing for the first book and 10p per copy for each additional book.